CLUELESS TO CONFIDENT

TALES OF TRIAL AND TRIUMPH IN MY TWENTIES

KHUSHIE RANDERIA

ISBN
Paperback 979-8-89632-755-4
Hardcase 979-8-89929-944-5

This book is dedicated to my parents, whose countless sacrifices and endless love have shaped every part of who I am. Your love, strength, and principles have been the foundation on which I've built my life, and for that, I am forever grateful.

To my husband, Ryan – my steadfast partner, my best friend, and my greatest cheerleader. Thank you for your love, patience, and for being by my side through every trial and triumph. You've made this journey not only possible but meaningful.

And to my precious daughter, whose laughter and light remind me every day of the beauty of unconditional love. You are my heart and my inspiration, always.

Contents

Author's Biography

Khushie is a storyteller, wife, and mother who has learned to embrace the ups and downs of life with humour and grace. Raised in a conservative Indian family, she spent her twenties trying to figure out life, one misstep at a time – juggling career ambitions, personal struggles, and an evolving sense of identity. Her debut book, *Clueless to Confident: Tales of Trial and Triumph in My Twenties*, chronicles her often hilarious, sometimes heartbreaking, but always enlightening journey of self-discovery.

Drawing from personal experiences, Khushie delves into the highs and lows of relationships, friendships, career challenges, and spiritual transformation. What makes her writing stand out is her ability to balance humour with vulnerability, inviting readers into her world with a candidness that feels like chatting with an old friend over coffee. Her story of navigating the turbulent waters of her twenties, while still trying to stay true to herself, offers a raw and relatable reflection on modern-day adulthood.

Khushie's life today is a testament to growth and transformation. She is happily married to Ryan, her unwavering pillar of support, and together, they are raising their daughter, whose presence has deepened her understanding of unconditional love. Whether it's sharing life lessons, recalling misadventures, or reflecting on her relationship with God, Khushie writes with the hope that her readers will laugh, cry, and find comfort in knowing they are not alone in the messy, beautiful chaos of life.

Outside of writing, Khushie is a passionate coach and a champion for personal growth and transformation. As an ICF-certified CCE life coach, mindfulness coach, NLP coach, and accomplished soft skills trainer, she has dedicated her career to empowering young adults and mothers to build mental and emotional resilience. Khushie's mission extends beyond storytelling; she actively mentors individuals to overcome challenges, embrace their authentic selves, and thrive in every aspect of life. A devoted wife and mother, she draws inspiration from her family and personal journey, infusing her work with relatable wisdom and genuine compassion. She enjoys travelling, quality time with family, and the little moments of joy that make life extraordinary. *Clueless to Confident: Tales of Trial and Triumph in My Twenties* is just the beginning of her journey as an author, with many more stories and lessons yet to share.

Preface

<hr>

Growing up in a conservative Indian family, I always felt like I was navigating two worlds. On one side was my family, deeply rooted in tradition and expectations, with my father—a strict, principled man—at the helm. He had a clear vision for my future, one that was safe, secure, and, most importantly, aligned with the values of our culture. My mother, on the other hand, was my quiet pillar of strength, supporting me in ways that often went unnoticed but were deeply felt. And then there was my elder brother, the rebel who always seemed to get away with breaking any rule.

As I stepped into my twenties, I found myself caught between the life that was planned for me and the life I secretly yearned for. I was clueless, to say the least. The world outside our home was vast and confusing, filled with opportunities and challenges that I was neither prepared for nor fully understood. Yet, with each misstep and each victory, I began to carve out my own path, learning and unlearning along the way.

This book is a collection of those lessons—moments of trial and triumph that transformed me from a directionless young adult into a more confident, self-assured individual. It's a story of rebellion and reconciliation, of making mistakes and making amends. But most importantly, it's a story of finding the courage to be true to myself in a world that often demands conformity.

As you read these tales, I hope you'll find parts of your own story in mine. Whether you are standing at the crossroads of a decision, grappling with expectations, or simply trying to figure out who you are, know that you are not alone. The journey from clueless to confident is one we all must take, and it's filled with more twists and turns than we could ever imagine.

Welcome to my story.

Foreword

It is my great pleasure to introduce you to Mrs Khushie Randeria, who was previously Miss Khushie Contractor when my wife and I were first introduced to her about 8 years ago. As a mentor and friend, it's been my joy and privilege to walk this inspiring journey with her. It's been an honour to witness and be a testament to her remarkable transformation, which has been beautifully captured in these pages.

When we met Khushie, she came across as an outgoing person who loved life and was eager to try new things. She was not one to think twice; at times, her impulsiveness got her into tight spots, but she always had a smile on her face, loved her family and friends, and enjoyed going on adventures. She showed strong leadership qualities, a hunger to learn, and demonstrated a teachable spirit. However, what truly stood out about her was her faith and love for God, her Saviour.

I commend Khushie for her courage in sharing her journey through her 20s. Her openness and honesty as she reflects on her mistakes, challenges, victories, and moments of doubt and fear are truly inspiring. Her story is a powerful testament to the strength of faith and the transformative power of God's love. It's a story that will inspire and motivate, showing that one can overcome any obstacle with faith and determination. Her journey is one that many of us can relate to, making her story all the more powerful.

For the past twenty-plus years, I have been working as a mentor and counsellor with young people, especially those between the ages of 18 and 35. I have seen and heard firsthand all the challenges they face, such as careers, love, friendship, family issues, and their spiritual journey, as they enter this age bracket.

This book is a comforting companion for young people about to enter their 20s and beyond. It's a reminder that you are not alone in your journey. It may make you laugh, shed a few tears, and most importantly, offer profound wisdom and invaluable guidance as you navigate the challenges and joys of this evolving period in your lives.

Pastor Daniel John

Counsellor and Executive Pastor of New Life Centre.

Life's challenges can often feel insurmountable, especially when shadowed by depression, anxiety, and the pain of broken relationships. In this deeply personal account, *Clueless to Confident: Tales of Trial and Triumph in My Twenties*, a young Parsi, Khushie Randeria, shares her journey through despair, offering an honest reflection on her struggles and the extraordinary transformation that followed.

At the heart of her story lies a life-changing encounter with Jesus Christ—a moment that reshaped her faith, her purpose, and ultimately her entire life. What began as a season of anguish became a journey of renewal, as she found strength in her newfound faith and courage to embrace profound change.

This book is more than a testament to resilience; it is a beacon of hope for anyone seeking light amidst darkness. It reminds us that even in our lowest moments, grace can find us, and healing is always possible.

In these pages, you will find an account of individual struggle but also a testament to resilience and the power of faith. This story is one of courage—not just the courage to confront pain and loss but the courage to choose change, to surrender to the unknown, and to embrace a life that is reborn in spirit and purpose.

For those who have wrestled with their own shadows, who have questioned their place in this world, or who are simply in search of a narrative that inspires hope, *Clueless to Confident: Tales of Trial and Triumph in My Twenties* will be a companion. It speaks to the universal human condition while offering a deeply personal testimony of transformation.

As you turn these pages, may you find encouragement, hope, and perhaps even the seeds of your own renewal. This is not just one woman's story; it is a testament to the transformative power of faith and the light that can emerge even in the darkest of times.

May Khushie's story inspire you, comfort you, and encourage you to believe in the transformative power of faith, helping you heal and learn to hope again.

– Katherine Abraham

Rex Karmaveer Awardee 2023-24

Legal Journalist

Acknowledgements

Writing this book has been one of the most transformative experiences of my life, and it would not have been possible without the unwavering support and love of the incredible people in my life.

First and foremost, to my amazing husband, Ryan. You have been my rock, my cheerleader, and my constant source of strength. Through the highs and lows, you have stood by my side, and I cannot thank you enough for being the best husband anyone could ask for. Your belief in me, your patience, and your unwavering love have been the pillars that held me up during this journey. Thank you for always being there, for making me laugh when I needed it the most, and for encouraging me to pursue my dreams.

To my beautiful daughter, who has taught me what unconditional love truly means. Your presence in my life has brought me immense joy, and you continue to inspire me every single day. Watching you grow, learn, and thrive has been one of my greatest blessings. You have shown me a kind of love I never knew existed, and for that, I am eternally grateful.

A heartfelt thank you to my parents. Your endless sacrifices and the lessons you've instilled in me have shaped the person I am today. I may not have acknowledged it enough, but your hard work, love, and dedication have never gone unnoticed. From the values you've taught me to the countless ways you've supported me, I owe so much of my strength, resilience, and success to you. Thank you for everything you've done and will continue to do.

To my mother-in-law, Behzad, thank you for being my driving force. Your encouragement has pushed me beyond what I thought I was capable of, and your belief in me has been a guiding light. You have always urged me to chase my dreams with full force, and for that, I am forever grateful. Your wisdom, kindness, and support have meant the world to me, and I'm incredibly lucky to have you in my life.

A special thanks to the entire team at Notion Press, who have been instrumental in bringing this project to life. Your professionalism, dedication, and expertise have made this journey smooth and enjoyable. Thank you for guiding me through this process with patience and precision, and for helping turn my vision into reality.

Lastly, to my mentor PDJ, who has always been a support and to everyone who has been a part of this journey, thank you you for your love, support, and belief in me. This book is a culmination of the lessons I've learned, the people who've shaped me, and the experiences that have defined me. I'm deeply grateful to all of you.

Introduction

When I was a child, the world seemed so simple. My days were filled with school, play, and the innocent belief that life was fair. I grew up in a conservative Zoroastrian Indian household, where traditions were valued, respect for elders was paramount, and the word of my father was law. My father was strict, a man of principles and many expectations. He believed in discipline, in the importance of family honour, and in a clear distinction between what was right and wrong. My elder brother, on the other hand, was a rebel. He was everything I was not allowed to be. He was free, carefree even, making his own choices and often breaking the rules that bound me. This polarity in our upbringing always puzzled me.

As a girl, I was expected to be obedient, to follow the rules, and to uphold the family's honour in ways my brother was never asked to. It was a burden I bore in silence, even though it never seemed fair. My mother, on the other hand, was my quiet ally in this. She loved me unconditionally, supporting me in ways that often went unnoticed by others but meant the world to me. She understood the unspoken struggles of being the 'good daughter,' and in her own way, she tried to shield me from the harshness of the world outside and the rigid expectations within our home.

Growing up in this environment has shaped who I am today. It taught me resilience, the importance of self-discipline, and the art of navigating a world filled with contradictions. But it also left me with a deep sense of confusion and frustration, especially as I transitioned from the protected world of childhood into the bewildering realm of adulthood.

This book, ***Clueless to Confident: Tales of Trials & Triumph in My Twenties***, is a reflection of that journey—a journey that took me from the safety of my conservative upbringing to the unpredictable, and often unforgiving, world of adulthood. It is a collection of stories, lessons, and experiences that have shaped me, challenged me, and ultimately helped me find my way.

The transition from adolescence to adulthood is a universally perplexing experience. For me, it was particularly jarring. My early twenties were a time of newfound freedom, and with that freedom came a series of trials—many of which I was ill-prepared for. I was suddenly thrust into situations where I had to make decisions on my own, navigate complex relationships, and face the realities of life head-on. There were moments of triumph, yes, but also moments of failure—times when I questioned everything I thought I knew.

One of the biggest challenges I faced was reconciling the expectations of my family with the person I was becoming. The values I had grown up with sometimes clashed with the realities of the world outside my home. I found myself constantly walking a tightrope, trying to balance the need to be a dutiful daughter with the desire to forge my path. It was a delicate dance, one that required a great deal of introspection and, at times, compromise.

My brother's influence also loomed large during these years. Watching him live his life on his own terms made me question why I couldn't do the same. But every time I tried to break free from the mould, I was reminded of my role as the obedient daughter, the one who had to uphold the family's honour. This internal conflict became a recurring theme in my life, one that I would have to confront time and time again.

Throughout these trials, my mother remained a constant source of support. She was my confidante, the person I turned to when the weight of expectations became too much to bear. She understood the pressures I faced, even if she didn't always agree with my choices. Her quiet strength and unwavering love gave me the courage to keep going, even when the path ahead seemed uncertain.

As I navigated through these years, I began to realise that the journey to adulthood is not about having all the answers – it's about learning, growing, and sometimes failing. It's about embracing the uncertainty and finding your way, even when the road ahead is unclear. It's about making mistakes, owning up to them, and using them as stepping stones to become a better version of yourself.

This book is not just a recounting of the events of my twenties; it is a testament to the resilience of the human spirit.

It is about the lessons learned along the way—the lessons of humility, strength, and perseverance. It is about finding confidence in the face of uncertainty and learning to trust yourself, even when the world around you seems to be falling apart.

In writing this book, I hope to offer a sense of affinity to those who may be going through similar struggles. The twenties are often painted as a time of freedom and discovery, but they can also be a time of confusion, fear, and self-doubt. It's easy to feel lost, to feel like you are the only one who doesn't have it all figured out. But the truth is, no one really does. We're all just doing the best we can with the cards we've been dealt.

If there's one thing I've learned from this journey, it's that life is a series of trials and triumphs, of highs and lows, of successes and failures. And that's okay. It's all part of the process of becoming who you are meant to be. The key is to keep moving forward, to keep learning, and to keep believing in yourself, even when things don't go as planned.

To anyone reading this, especially those in their twenties, I want you to know that it's okay to be clueless at times. It's okay to feel like you don't have all the answers. What matters is that you keep going, that you keep striving to become the best version of yourself. And along the way, don't forget to celebrate your triumphs, no matter how small, and learn from your trials, no matter how difficult.

As you embark on your own journey through life, remember that every experience, whether good or bad, is an opportunity for growth. Embrace the trials, cherish the triumphs, and above all, trust yourself. You are stronger and more capable than you know, and with each step you take, you are moving closer to the person you are meant to be.

This book reflects my journey—from clueless to confident. I hope it serves as a reminder that you are not alone in your struggles and that, no matter how challenging life may seem, there's always a way forward. Here's to the trials, the triumphs, and everything in between. May your journey be as fulfilling as mine has been, and may you find the confidence to face whatever comes your way.

What Can You Expect from This Book?

Well, for starters, you'll get a front-row seat to some of the most ridiculous situations I found myself in. Like the time I ignored every red flag in a relationship because I was too busy convincing myself that it was "meant to be" (spoiler: it wasn't). You'll also get a glimpse into the weird and wonderful world of navigating career choices, friendships, and the occasional quarter-life crisis.

But it's not all just about me. This book is also about you. It's about the universal experience of being in your twenties and feeling like everyone else has it together while you are just trying to figure out which way is up. It's about finding confidence in the chaos, learning to laugh at yourself, and realising that no one really knows what they're doing—we're all just pretending to be adults.

So, if you are ready to dive into a world of awkward moments, hard-earned lessons, and a healthy dose of humour, then grab a cup of tea (or something stronger, no judgement here), and let's get started. By the end of this book, you might not have all the answers, but you'll at least know that you are not alone in the struggle. And who knows? You might even feel a little more confident about this whole adulting thing—or at the very least, you'll have a few good laughs along the way.

Welcome to the club, fellow clueless twenty-somethings. I hope my story inspires you to embrace your own.

Chapter 1

Faking Adulthood: The Transition from A Teenager to An Adult

In her twenties, she danced through freedom's door,

With hearts in her hands, she sought something more.

She stumbled through love in a whirlwind of grace,

Blind to the red flags, she quickened her pace.

Her laughter turned to tears as lessons unfurled,

In the chaos of youth, a new wisdom swirled.

Through heartbreak and struggle, she learned to be wise,

Emerging from trials with clearer, braver eyes.

The moment I turned twenty, I had this grand vision of adulthood. It was supposed to be a seamless transition where I would magically acquire all the wisdom and sophistication that grown-ups seemed to have. Spoiler alert: that didn't happen. Instead, I found myself in a strange new world, armed with a newfound sense of freedom and absolutely no idea what to do with it.

Suddenly, I could make my own decisions—how exhilarating! I could eat ice cream for dinner if I wanted, stay out till 10 pm, and finally have the independence I had long craved. But here's the thing about freedom: it comes with a side of responsibility. And responsibility, as I quickly learned, is not nearly as fun as it sounds.

With this freedom came the opportunity to forge new friendships, which I did with great enthusiasm. I was convinced that the more friends I had, the more adult I would appear. So, I surrounded myself with a motley crew of characters—each one more interesting than the last. There was the friend who could sweet-talk their way out of anything, the one who always knew where the best parties were (you know what kind of parties I'm talking about), and, of course, the one who perpetually had a new life crisis that required immediate attention. Looking back, I can't help but marvel at the fact that I thought this was what adult friendships were supposed to be like. I mean, who needed stability and mutual respect when you could have drama and chaos, right?

Matters of the Heart (and Other Organs)

Then there were the relationships. Ah, the relationships. If only someone had handed me a guidebook titled, "How to Spot Red Flags Before You End Up in a Soup." But no, I ignored the flashing neon signs that screamed "Danger!" and marched right into situations that would make even the most dramatic of Bollywood films look tame. My romantic life was less of a fairy tale and more of a Hindi Soap Opera, one directed by Ekta Kapoor. But, hey, what's youth without a few cringe-worthy love stories, right? But here's the funny thing about ignoring red flags—they don't just go away. They pile up, one on top of the other, until you are buried under a mountain of issues that are impossible to ignore. And when that mountain finally collapses, as it inevitably does, you are left with two options: blame the world for being unfair, or realise that maybe, just maybe, you've been doing this whole adulthood thing wrong.

Well, I decided to blame the world. Now, when it comes to relationships, let's just say I was a hopeless romantic who wore my heart on my sleeve. The moment a guy showed even the slightest interest in me, I was already imagining our future together—complete with a house, two kids, and a dog. Subtlety was not my strong suit. I was the kind of person who jumped into the deep end of the relationship pool without checking if there was any water.

And, of course, this enthusiasm led to some rather... complicated situations. Like the time I ended up dating two guys at the same time—without realising it, of course. One minute, I was swept off my feet by a charming smile, and the next, I was equally enchanted by another. Somehow, in my naive eagerness to find "the one" (you will read more about this in the upcoming chapters), I had managed to entangle myself in a love triangle of my own making. It was the kind of situation that would have made for a great rom-com if it weren't happening to me.

Needless to say, it didn't take long for the whole thing to blow up in my face. Trying to juggle two relationships at once was like trying to balance on a tightrope with a hurricane blowing – it was only a matter of time before I fell, and when I did, I fell hard. The embarrassment, the awkward conversations, the mess I had created – it was a royal disaster.

The One That Got Away

Amidst all these romantic misadventures was my best friend, (Let's call him Rahul). We had grown up together, sharing everything from lunchboxes to our deepest secrets. He was my rock, my confidant, the one person who always had my back no matter how ridiculous my latest crisis was.

But here's where my immaturity and selfishness reared their ugly heads. Rahul had feelings for me—real, genuine feelings that went beyond friendship. And me? I consistently relegated him to the infamous friend zone, all while venting to him about my latest dating disasters. Talk about irony.

Our friendship became a complicated tangle of unspoken emotions and missed signals. I took his presence and unwavering support for granted, assuming he'd always be there no matter how much I ignored or downplayed his feelings. It was toxic and unfair, and I was too wrapped up in my own drama to see the damage I was causing.

Eventually, Rahul had had enough. He confronted me, laying his heart bare and expressing how much my actions had hurt him over the years. I wish I could say I handled it gracefully, but in truth, I was defensive and dismissive, unwilling to face the consequences of my actions.

Shortly after, Rahul accepted a job offer abroad and moved halfway across the world. Just like that, I lost over ten years of friendship due to my own selfishness and immaturity. The void he left was immense, and it took me a long time to come to terms with the fact that I was the one responsible for pushing away one of the most important people in my life. I often think about him and wish to reconnect with him. However, I have never gained the courage to do so. Well, perhaps that's a lesson I'm yet to learn.

But as messy as it was, it was a turning point. I learned that love isn't something to rush into just because you are afraid of being alone or eager to feel grown up. Sometimes, the best thing you can do is slow down, take a breath, and wait for the right person to come along—without dragging someone else into your confusion.

The Weight of Expectations

As if navigating the choppy waters of relationships wasn't challenging enough, I was also in the throes of preparing for competitive exams. In my family, education was non-negotiable, and excellence was expected, and that pressure weighed on me like a ton of bricks.

But here's the thing about emotional baggage: it doesn't simply disappear when you bury it under a mountain of textbooks. I tried to drown out the heartache from my failed relationships and the suffocating environment at home by throwing myself into my studies. I convinced myself that if I just worked hard enough, I could outrun the anxiety and depression that were quietly gnawing away at me.

Unfortunately, that's not how life works. The more I tried to ignore my emotional pain, the more it found ways to manifest. As a teenager, I had developed a habit of hurting myself—a behaviour that started as a misguided attempt to grab attention and evoke sympathy from my friends. What began as an immature cry for help soon spiralled into an unhealthy coping mechanism. Instead of facing my mental and emotional struggles head-on, I reverted to physical pain as an outlet.

It became a secret addiction, something I could control when everything else in my life felt chaotic and overwhelming. But deep down, I knew it was a dangerous cycle—one that only pushed me further into a dark, lonely place. The pressure to succeed academically, combined with the turmoil of my personal life, created a perfect storm of anxiety and depression that I was ill-equipped to handle.

A Lesson in Humility

Just when I thought my life was an endless cycle of self-inflicted chaos, life decided to give me a much-needed reality check in the form of a Christmas programme for underprivileged children. A group of us decided it would be a good idea to spread some holiday cheer, and off we went with our Santa hats and candy canes, thinking we were doing something incredibly noble.

I had spent the entire morning agonising over what to wear—after all, even charity work required the perfect outfit, right? I tried on half my wardrobe, grumbling about not having enough clothes and critiquing myself in the mirror as if I were preparing for a Vogue photoshoot. Priorities, clearly.

As we arrived at the community, the stark contrast between my world and theirs was impossible to ignore. We were invited into a small hut where a family of eight lived—yes, eight people in a space smaller than my bedroom. The youngest girl, probably no more than ten years old, immediately caught my attention. She was all smiles, her eyes sparkling with a joy that seemed too big for her tiny frame.

After the festivities, as we were preparing to leave, I noticed this little girl pause at a small 5-inch rectangular mirror hanging crookedly on the wall. She glanced at herself, smoothed down her hair, flashed a radiant smile, and skipped out to wave us goodbye. That simple act hit me harder than any of my previous blunders.

Here was a girl who had so little by material standards, yet exuded pure happiness and confidence. Meanwhile, I had spent the day fretting over my outfit and obsessing about my appearance, completely oblivious to how privileged I truly was. Humility washed over me like a cold shower, awakening me to the shallow and self-absorbed path I had been treading.

That moment was a turning point. It made me realise that adulthood isn't about the freedom to make careless choices or accumulate experiences for the sake of it. It's about growing into a person who appreciates what they have, learns from their mistakes, and strives to be better—not just for themselves but for those around them. That day, I learned a lesson in humility that no textbook could have taught me. The image of that little girl, smiling at herself in that tiny mirror, will forever be etched in my memory—a reminder that true beauty and contentment come from within, and that I had a lot of growing up to do.

Embracing The Messy Journey

After stumbling through friendships that left me drained and relationships that ended in spectacular fashion, I finally had to face the truth: I wasn't as grown up as I thought I was. Adulthood wasn't about having the freedom to do whatever I wanted—it was about having the wisdom to know what I should do. It was about making choices that were good for me, even if they weren't always the most fun. And it was about admitting that I didn't have all the answers and that it was okay to ask for help when I needed it.

Faking adulthood had been a wild ride, full of laughter, tears, and more than a few embarrassing moments. But it taught me one of the most important lessons of my twenties: that humility is the key to truly growing up. It's what allows us to learn from our mistakes, to admit when we're wrong, and to move forward with a little more grace and a lot more wisdom.

My early twenties were a chaotic blend of misadventures, heartbreaks, and humbling experiences. I stumbled, fell, and made a complete fool of myself more times than I can count. But through it all, I learned invaluable lessons about love, friendship, and the kind of person I wanted to become.

Faking adulthood taught me that it's okay not to have everything figured out, that making mistakes is part of the journey, and that sometimes, the most profound lessons come from the most unexpected places. I learned the importance of treating people with kindness and respect, valuing the relationships that truly matter, and finding joy and gratitude in the simple things.

So, here's to faking adulthood—because, let's be honest, we're all just figuring it out as we go. And if we're lucky, we'll stumble upon moments that steer us in the right direction, reminding us of what being an adult is all about.

A Note from Present Me to the 20-Year-Old Me

Dear 20-Something-Year-Old Me,

You're standing on the edge of adulthood, thinking you've got it all figured out. Spoiler alert—you don't. But that's okay. None of us really do at that age, and the beauty of this phase is in the lessons you're about to learn, even if they come wrapped in the messy, sometimes painful package of experience.

Remember that sudden rush of freedom when you first started navigating the adult world? It felt like someone handed you the keys to the kingdom, and you were ready to conquer it all. You'll dive headfirst into friendships, relationships, and a whirlwind of new experiences. But, with that freedom comes responsibility, and that's where things get tricky.

You're going to make mistakes, big ones. You'll wear your heart on your sleeve and jump into relationships with anyone who shows you the slightest bit of interest. You'll think you've found love, but more often than not, you'll find yourself tangled in complicated situations—like the time you ended up dating two people at once and royally messed things up. It's going to be a tough lesson, but it's one you need to learn.

And then there's the friend you've had for years, the one you kept in the friend zone, never realising how much you were hurting him. Your love triangles and inability to see what was right in front of you will cost you that friendship. Losing him will sting, and you'll carry that regret with you. It's a painful reminder that relationships, whether romantic or platonic, require honesty and clarity—things you're still figuring out.

You'll also try to bury your heartache and escape the pressures at home by diving into your studies and pursuing competitive exams. But the strict environment at home, combined with the anxiety and depression you're battling, will make it hard to focus. You'll turn to self-harm as a way to cope, thinking that the physical pain is easier to deal with than the emotional turmoil inside you. It's a dark path, and it will feel like an addiction, but this too is part of your journey.

But amidst all the chaos, there will be moments that open your eyes. Like the Christmas programme you joined for underprivileged children, where you visited a tiny hut filled with a family of eight. The youngest girl, full of smiles, will glance at herself in a small, five-inch mirror before leaving, completely content with what she sees. That moment will hit you like a ton of bricks. You'll realise how often you've been consumed with trivial worries about your appearance or your possessions, and you'll begin to understand the value of humility and gratitude.

So, here's my advice to you: Don't be too hard on yourself for the mistakes you'll make. They're part of the process, part of growing up. You're learning what it means to be an adult, and that's a messy, imperfect journey. Every wrong turn teaches you something valuable. You'll learn about humility, about the importance of honesty in relationships, and about how to start taking responsibility for your own happiness.

You're faking adulthood now, but trust me, you'll get the hang of it eventually. And when you do, you'll look back and see that every stumble along the way was leading you to the person you're becoming.

Keep going, keep learning, and don't be afraid to admit when you don't have all the answers.

With love and wisdom from the future,

Your Present Self

Chapter 2

Self-discovery And Identity: Lessons Learned About Myself, Values and Principles

In search of herself, she reached for the sky,
Amid self-doubt and fears, she learned to rely.
With faith as her guide, she found peace within,
A higher purpose emerged from the chaos and din.
Through shadows of struggle, her spirit would soar,
Embracing new values she never knew before.
With God as her compass, she faced her deep strife,
And blossomed into the woman who reclaimed her own life.

The Beginning of The Journey

The journey of self-discovery is often romanticised as a path filled with enlightening moments and peaceful self-reflection. But for me, it was anything but peaceful. It was a journey filled with internal battles, moments of despair, and a constant tug-of-war between the person I was and the person I wanted to become. As I delved deeper into my twenties, I realised that finding oneself isn't about becoming someone new but rather uncovering the person you've always been beneath the layers of societal expectations, emotional baggage, and self-imposed limitations.

The Search for Self: Confronting My Inner Demons

In my early twenties, I was living a life that was far from authentic. I had become adept at wearing masks—masks that reflected the person I thought I needed to be to gain acceptance from others. Whether it was being the overachiever, the dutiful daughter, or the perfect friend, I was constantly playing roles that left me feeling hollow. I was disconnected from my true self, and this disconnection manifested in ways that were both destructive and self-sabotaging.

My relationships were shallow and unfulfilling, my academic achievements felt empty, and my sense of self-worth was tied to external validation. I was constantly seeking approval, be it from friends, family, or even strangers. No amount of praise or recognition could fill the void inside me. I was living a lie, and the deeper I went down this path, the more I lost touch with who I really was. I was purposeless. There were mornings when I woke up, thinking, "What if my whole life is just a long, never-ending nightmare? A dream that I would wake up from and breathe a sigh of relief (hopefully I wouldn't make the same mistakes again, or maybe I will)."

The Breaking Point: When The Facade Cracked

The breaking point came when the facade I had so carefully constructed began to crack. The lack of peace in my life became unbearable. I was constantly anxious, plagued by thoughts of inadequacy, and overwhelmed by a sense of impending doom. My addiction to self-harm, which had started as a misguided attempt to cope with emotional pain, had now become a full-blown obsession.

Each cut, each burn, was a twisted way of punishing myself for not being good enough. It was as if I believed that by inflicting physical pain, I could somehow atone for my perceived failures. But the truth was, no amount of self-inflicted pain could ever erase the emotional scars that were driving me to these extreme measures.

The saddest part was that my friends knew, but it was a fashion statement more than a cry for help. Self-harm had suddenly become the new style statement or fad. Looking back, I wish someone had rigorously shaken me and told me that I needed to work on my mental health.

Battling the Old Me: The Temptation to Relapse

As I began to explore the possibility of change, I found myself caught between two opposing forces: the old me, who was entrenched in self-destructive habits, and the new me, who longed for something better. The battle was fierce, and there were times when the old me seemed to have the upper hand.

The temptation to relapse into old habits was always there, lurking in the background. On some days, the urge to hurt myself was so strong that it felt like a physical force, pulling me back into the darkness. I would find myself standing in front of the mirror, holding a blade, ready to give in to the familiar pain that had become my coping mechanism.

But in those moments, I would also hear a whisper—a voice inside me that urged me to resist, to fight the urge and rely on something greater than myself. That voice, which I came to recognise as God's, became my lifeline in those moments of despair.

A Leap of Faith: Finding Jesus in My Struggles

It was during one of these dark moments that I had a dream that would change the course of my life. In this dream, my life was in shambles—I was struggling, drowning in my insecurities, and completely lost. The pain and turmoil were overwhelming, and I felt like I was being pulled under by the weight of it all.

But then, out of nowhere, someone appeared. He was riding a white horse, a knight in shining armour, and there was something about him that radiated strength and peace. He reached out his hand to me and said, "I am Jesus, take my hand and I will give you peace."

In that moment, I didn't hesitate. I didn't question or doubt. I simply took a leap of faith and accepted the help that was being offered to me. It was as if, for the first time, I truly understood what it meant to surrender, to trust in something greater than myself.

When I woke up, I felt a sense of calm that I hadn't experienced in years. The dream had been so vivid, so real, that I couldn't shake the feeling that it was more than just a figment of my imagination. It was a message, a promise that if I trusted in Jesus, I would find the peace I was searching for.

The Struggle Continues: Wrestling With Old Habits

Despite this profound experience, my struggles didn't disappear overnight. The battle between the old me and the new me continued, and there were times when I faltered. The urge to hurt myself was still there, and there were moments when I gave in, succumbing to the temporary relief that self-harm provided.

But each time I relapsed, the guilt and shame weighed heavier on me. I began to realise that every time I broke my promise to myself—and to Jesus—I was undermining the very peace I was trying to achieve. The internal conflict was exhausting, and I knew that something had to change.

Moments of Triumph: Learning to Trust in Jesus

Over time, I began to experience moments of triumph—small victories where I resisted the urge to hurt myself and instead turned to Jesus for strength. These moments were empowering and reinforced the belief that I was capable of change.

I started to see that the key to overcoming my addiction wasn't just about willpower; it was about learning to trust in something greater than myself. I realised that I didn't have to face my struggles alone—that Jesus was there, guiding me, even in my darkest moments.

Letting Go of Toxic Friendships: A Necessary Step in My Journey

As I grew closer to Jesus and began changing myself, I started to see my life in a new light. The things that once seemed so important began to fade away, and I realised that some of the people I had surrounded myself with were holding me back. My friendships, which I had once thought were so vital, were revealed to be toxic and draining.

Slowly, I began to distance myself from these toxic relationships. It wasn't an easy decision, but it was a necessary one. I had to let go of the people who were contributing to my pain and who couldn't support the person I was becoming. Automatically, my group of friends began to shrink, and I was left with just a handful of people who truly mattered.

At first, my remaining friends didn't understand why I was changing so much. They found it weird and even questioned my decisions. But as they saw the positive changes in me – how I was happier, more peaceful, and finally starting to see my own worth – they began to respect me in a way they hadn't before. This newfound respect from those who remained in my life was both comforting and validating.

Through this tough process of weaning off toxic relationships, my best friend Meher was the glue that held my world together. Meher is the kind of person who lights up any room she walks into, with her loud, bubbly personality and infectious energy. She has an extraordinary ability to see the best in people, always offering a kind word or a forgiving heart. Her giddy-headed nature adds a layer of charm—she's the friend who can laugh at the world, herself, and any predicament she finds herself in, often with a shrug and a smile.

For 25 years, we've been inseparable, more like sisters than friends. If we were cartoon characters, Meher would undoubtedly be the one getting into all sorts of mischief, calling me to clean up her messes—hence her affectionate nickname for me, her "fire extinguisher." Despite all her wild, carefree ways, she's a constant source of joy and loyalty in my life, always reminding me that laughter and love can be found even in the most chaotic of times.

The Final Battle: Making A Promise I Wouldn't Break

As my journey progressed, I reached a point where I realised that no matter how tempted I got, I had to stop hurting myself. The physical pain was no longer a viable outlet for my emotional suffering, and I knew that I had to find healthier ways to cope.

But more than that, I began to understand the importance of being true to the promises I made—especially the ones I made to Jesus. Breaking those promises not only hurt me but also distanced me from the peace and healing that I was seeking. I realised that in order to truly change, I had to honour my word.

One day, after a particularly intense struggle, I made a promise to Jesus – a promise that I never wanted to break. I vowed that I would never hurt myself again, that I would find other ways to cope with my pain, and that I would trust in Jesus to help me through the difficult times.

The Power of a Promise: Staying True to My Word

Keeping that promise wasn't easy. There were times when the urge to relapse was overwhelming, when the old habits threatened to resurface. But each time, I reminded myself of the promise I had made, and I turned to Jesus for strength. I prayed for the courage to stay true to my word, and slowly, I began to see that it was possible.

The more I honoured my promise, the stronger I became. I started to see that my worth wasn't tied to my ability to endure pain, but rather to my ability to overcome it. I learned that true strength wasn't about how much I could suffer, but about how much I could heal.

Transformation: Becoming The Person I Was Meant to Be

As I continued to keep my promise, I noticed a profound shift in my life. The battles between the old me and the new me became less frequent, and the moments of triumph became more consistent. I began to see myself not as a victim of my circumstances, but as someone who had the power to change and grow.

My faith became the cornerstone of my identity, the foundation upon which I built my new life. It gave me the strength to overcome my self-destructive habits, to confront my anxiety and depression head-on, and to embrace the person I was becoming. I found my worth in Jesus.

But perhaps the most important lesson I learned was the value of staying true to my word. By keeping my promise to Jesus, I discovered a sense of integrity and self-respect that I had never known before. I realised that my worth wasn't determined by external factors, but by my ability to live in alignment with my values and beliefs.

Family and Faith: Navigating the Challenges

While my personal transformation was deeply rewarding, it also presented new challenges, particularly within my family. Coming from an orthodox, traditional background (not

Christianity), I knew that my newfound faith wouldn't be easily accepted. My family had certain expectations of me, and I was afraid that revealing my spiritual journey would lead to conflict and misunderstanding.

So, I kept my faith hidden from them, not out of shame, but out of a desire to maintain peace. I constantly prayed for the courage to share my faith openly because I wanted them to experience the same peace and transformation that I had found. However, I knew that the best thing I could do was let my changed behaviour be my testament.

By living in alignment with my faith and values, I hoped to show my family the positive changes that had taken place in my life. I wanted them to see that my faith had made me a better person—happier, more peaceful, and more fulfilled.

Lessons Learned: The Power of Faith and Integrity

Looking back, I realise that this period of self-discovery was one of the most transformative times of my life. It taught me the importance of faith, not just in Jesus, but in myself and in the journey I was on. I learned that my true identity wasn't something that could be dictated by others—it was something I had to uncover through my own experiences, values, and passions.

I also learned the power of surrender, of letting go of the need to control everything and trusting that there is a greater plan at work. It was a humbling lesson, but one that brought me the peace and clarity I had been searching for all along.

In the end, my search for self led me to find Jesus, and in finding Jesus, I found myself. It was a journey that was as painful as it was beautiful, and one that I wouldn't trade for anything.

Moving Forward with Faith and Purpose

As I continue on my journey, I carry with me the lessons I've learned about faith, identity, and integrity. I know that there will be challenges ahead, but I also know that I have the strength and the faith to overcome them. My promise to Jesus remains my guiding light, reminding me of the power of staying true to my word and the importance of living in alignment with my values.

This journey of self-discovery and identity is ongoing, but I'm no longer afraid of what lies ahead. I know that with Jesus by my side, I can face whatever comes my way with courage, faith, and a sense of purpose.

A Note from Present Me to the 20-Year-Old Me

Dear 20-Something-Year-Old Me,

You're about to embark on one of the most challenging yet rewarding journeys of your life—the journey of self-discovery. I know you're feeling lost, burdened by anxiety, depression, and a deep sense of dissatisfaction with who you are. It's like you're standing at a crossroads, unsure of which path to take, but let me assure you, what's coming next will shape you in ways you can't even imagine.

You're searching for peace, for a way out of the darkness that seems to have settled over your life. You're battling an addiction to self-harm, using physical pain to mask the emotional turmoil you don't know how to handle. It's a lonely place to be, and I know how much you're struggling. But here's something you need to know—you don't have to do it alone. I see you trying to be strong, to find a way out on your own, but there's a greater strength that's waiting to lift you up if you just reach out for it.

This is the time when you'll start turning towards God, seeking something greater than yourself to make sense of the chaos. That search will lead you to an encounter that will change everything. In a dream, amidst all the pain and confusion, you'll see a figure—a knight in shining armour—riding in on a white horse. He'll offer you His hand, and with it, the promise of peace. You won't hesitate; you'll take that leap of faith, and it will be the beginning of your transformation.

As you grow closer to God, you'll begin to see yourself differently. The person you've been—wrapped up in self-doubt, insecurity, and pain—will start to fade as a new version of you emerges. But it won't be easy. You'll find yourself caught between the old you and the new you, battling the temptation to fall back into old habits. There will be times when you'll give in, but there will also be moments of triumph when you'll resist. Slowly, you'll learn the power of keeping your promises, especially the one you'll make to God to never hurt yourself again. It will be a promise you'll fight to keep, and it will teach you about resilience and the strength that comes from faith.

This journey will also mean letting go of certain people in your life. As you change, you'll realise that some friendships are holding you back, keeping you tied to a version of yourself that you're trying to leave behind. It will hurt to let go, but it's necessary for your growth. Your circle will shrink, but those who remain will respect and support the new you. They'll see the peace you've found, the confidence you're starting to build, and they'll come to understand and admire the person you're becoming.

At the same time, you'll face challenges at home. Your family, steeped in tradition and orthodoxy, won't understand your newfound faith. You'll have to hide it, to live with the tension of wanting to share this incredible transformation but knowing it won't be accepted. It will be frustrating, and at times you'll feel like you're living a double life. But remember, your actions speak louder than words. Let your changed behaviour be a testament to your faith. In time, they may not fully understand, but they'll see the positive impact it has had on you.

So, dear 20-Something-Year-Old Me, know that the pain you're feeling now is not the end of your story. It's the beginning of a journey towards discovering who you truly are, what you value, and the principles you'll build your life around. Embrace the changes, even when they're difficult. Trust in the process, and above all, hold on to your faith — it will guide you through the darkest moments and lead you to a place of peace and purpose.

With all the love and encouragement you need,

Your Future Self

Chapter 3

Relationships And Boundaries: Experiences with Friendships, Romantic Relationships, Breakups and Family Dynamics

In love and in friendships, her heart would confide,
Yet boundaries were blurred as she navigated the tide.
Through breakups and battles with family and friend,
She learned that true wisdom comes from how one can mend.
With each heartache and conflict, she found her own way,
Redefining her values with each passing day.
In letting go of the toxic, her strength was revealed,
Embracing the lessons that life had concealed.

The Friend Who Became My Anchor: A Spiritual Connection

In the midst of my spiritual journey, I encountered a friend who shared my faith and became a pivotal figure in my life.

Let's call him "Derek." Derek wasn't just a friend; he was someone who helped me grow spiritually and brought me closer to Jesus. He introduced me to his mentor, Pastor Daniel John (aka PDJ), who is wise and compassionate, and to a circle of youngsters who, like me, were navigating their faith in a world that often felt like it was going in the opposite direction. For the first time, I felt like I wasn't alone. Here was a judgement-free space where I could openly share my issues and struggles, and in return, I received the support I so desperately needed.

But life isn't always as simple as finding the right people at the right time. Derek and I grew closer, and soon, our friendship evolved into something more – a relationship. And like all relationships, ours too came with its own set of complications.

The Secret Relationship: Navigating Love in A Traditional Household

Being in a relationship with Derek was exhilarating but also filled with tension because it meant I had to keep it a secret from my family. In my conservative Indian household, dating was something that wasn't to be done unless marriage was on the horizon. And dating someone from another religion? That was an absolute no-no. For the longest time, I kept my relationship under wraps, skilfully dodging questions from my parents and pretending everything was business as usual.

My elder brother, who had an uncanny knack for sniffing out secrets, had a vague idea that something was up. But he always brushed it off as a passing phase, convinced that I wasn't serious about it. Little did he know that I was knee-deep in a relationship that came with its own set of challenges.

The Weight of Another's World: When Love and Substance Abuse Collide

Derek was a wonderful person. He was one of those rare individuals who seemed to embody all the qualities you'd want in a friend or partner. He was incredibly kind-hearted, the type of person who could brighten your day with just a smile and a kind word. Respectful in every sense of the word, he treated everyone with dignity and never crossed the line into negativity or abuse. What stood out most about Derek was his ability to always see the best in people, even when they couldn't see it in themselves. His patience was unmatched, making him a steady and reliable presence in the lives of those who knew him.

Hard work was second nature to Derek. He had a passion for music that drove him, a love for Jesus that fuelled his soul and gave him purpose. But Derek wasn't just about the present; he carried a past filled with challenges and battles that he had fought and won. Those experiences shaped him, making him even more determined in his quest to find and establish himself in life. He was on a journey, not just to succeed but to become the best version of himself, constantly evolving and growing, with the hope of leaving a positive impact on the world around him.

However, like all of us, he came with his own baggage. He occasionally struggled with an addiction to substance abuse, and soon enough, those issues began to spill over into our relationship. What started as a loving connection gradually turned into a burden that was too heavy for either of us to carry.

We were dating on and off, breaking up and getting back together more times than I could count. Each time we broke up, it felt like my world was crumbling, but the moment we patched things up, it was as if nothing had changed. But deep down, things had changed. His battles with this addiction became mine, and they started to take a toll on me. I was no longer just dealing with my own anxieties and struggles; I was also trying to hold together someone else's broken pieces.

It reached a point where PDJ, who had been guiding us both spiritually and personally, told us that we needed to end our relationship. For Derek and me, this was like a dagger to the heart. I didn't know if I could ever let go of him. I had prayed, hoping and knowing all of these years that he was the one. But the reality was staring us both in the face: we were hurting each other more than we were helping.

The Breakup Cycle: Love Triangles and Heartache

For about two years, Derek and I found ourselves in a toxic cycle of dating and breaking up so frequently that I lost track of how many times it happened. We had reached a point where even our friends looked at our breakups as a usual Monday. The relationship that once brought us joy was now a source of constant heartache. Every conversation seemed to end in a fight. We were both walking on eggshells, afraid of saying the wrong thing, yet somehow always ending up in an argument.

Ironically, my old self resurfaced; in my desperation to find love, the slightest attention from someone else would drift me in that direction. It wasn't intentional, but it happened nonetheless. I'd find myself in another love triangle, hurting not just Derek but also the new person and, of course, myself. Derek, on the other hand, was doing the same. We were both broken in our own ways, unable to see clearly through the fog of our pain.

In my heart of hearts, I only wanted to be with Derek because I didn't know who else would accept me with my faith and with all my flaws. I was afraid that I would never find someone who would understand me the way he did. Derek, on the other hand, believed that I would never leave him, no matter how badly we fought. We were both clinging to a relationship that was long past its expiration date, out of fear of being alone.

The Family Revelation: When Secrets Come Crashing Down

In a moment of desperation, after years of praying, I thought to myself, "What if I just told my parents the truth? Maybe if they knew about my faith and my relationship with Derek, they might accept it. Maybe things would be simpler."

As you can imagine, this didn't go down well. In fact, it was an absolute disaster. When I finally mustered up the courage to tell my parents, they were furious. My father's reaction was as explosive as a volcano, and my mother, who had always been my source of support, was devastated. My brother, who had always been somewhat protective of me, was beyond furious. He couldn't believe that I had been hiding something so significant from him.

I was forced to let go of my faith—or at least, that's what they wanted. But of course, I didn't. How could I? My faith was not my religion but a relationship. One I was never going to let go of; it was the only thing that had kept me afloat during some of the darkest times in my life. But now, I was being monitored by my brother, who seemed to have taken on the role of the family watchdog. Every move I made was scrutinised, and every friend I had was labelled a bad influence. My entire social circle was under suspicion, and I was isolated in a way that I had never experienced before.

The Aftermath: The Broken Relationship and Shattered Trust

My relationship with Derek was over. My mental health, already fragile, took a nosedive. The once strong and resilient girl I prided myself on being was now a shadow of her former self. I went from thinking, "He is the one," to convincing myself that I was destined to be single for the rest of my life.

Let's not forget the new title I had earned in my family: the black sheep. I was no longer the dutiful daughter who could do no wrong. Now, I was the one who had betrayed my family's trust, the one who had brought shame upon the household. My parents, who once praised me for my accomplishments, now looked at me with a mixture of disappointment and worry.

And as if that wasn't enough, my parents launched into "Operation Find a Suitable Boy." Suddenly, there was a sense of urgency that I had never seen before. Matrimonial ads, family friends, and distant relatives were all enlisted in the mission to find me a husband. The speed at which this was happening was dizzying. I went from being the independent woman with her own mind to being a commodity that needed to be "settled down" as soon as possible.

Finding Humour in The Chaos: The Unexpected Twist

Now, here's where things take a bit of a humorous twist. Looking back at the sheer absurdity of some of these situations, I can't help but laugh. For instance, my parents' attempts to find me a match were nothing short of comical. The criteria they came up with for the perfect husband were like something out of a Bollywood script. He had to be tall, fair, well-educated, come from a good family, and—this one still makes me chuckle—have no bad habits. In other words, they were looking for Mr. Perfect, who, as far as I'm concerned, doesn't exist.

Then there was the time I was set up on a blind date with a potential suitor. The poor guy showed up, all polished and ready to impress, while I was still reeling from my breakup with Derek. Needless to say, the date was a disaster. I spent the entire evening trying to avoid talking about anything personal, while he kept trying to steer the conversation towards marriage. By the end of the night, we both knew there was no way this was going to work out, and we parted ways with polite smiles and relieved sighs.

And let's not forget my brother's newfound role as my personal bodyguard. He took it upon himself to monitor my every move, which meant that even a simple outing with friends felt like a covert mission. I would sneak out to meet my friends, only to find him trailing behind me, making sure I wasn't up to any "mischief." It was like living in a spy movie, only without the cool gadgets or the thrill of adventure.

The Hard Lessons Learned: Boundaries, Self-Worth, and Moving On

Despite the chaos, the heartbreak, and the drama, I learned some invaluable lessons during this time. One of the most important lessons was about boundaries. I realised that in my desperation to find love and acceptance, I had allowed my boundaries to be crossed time and time again. Whether it was in my relationship with Derek or in my interactions with my family, I had given too much of myself away, and it had left me feeling empty and drained.

I also learned a hard lesson about self-worth. For so long, I had tied my sense of worth to my relationships, thinking that being loved by someone else would somehow validate me. But the truth is, self-worth comes from God. It's about recognising your own value, regardless of what others think or how they treat you.

And finally, I learned that sometimes, moving on is the best thing you can do for yourself. Letting go of Derek was one of the hardest things I've ever done, but it was also one of the most necessary. It allowed me to heal, to grow, and to start rebuilding my life on my own terms. Of course, by guarding my heart this time.

And as for the future? Well, I'm still figuring that out. But one thing's for sure: I'm no longer that girl who feels the need to hide who she is or what she believes in. I'm not perfect, but I'm learning to embrace the perfect journey that God has set out for me. And who knows? Maybe Mr. Perfect is out there somewhere, or maybe he isn't. But either way, I'm okay with it. After all, the most important relationship I've learned to nurture is the one I have with Jesus and myself.

As I sit here, reflecting on that tumultuous time in my life, fast forward five years, and Derek is now thriving. He fought his battle with substance abuse head-on and came out on the other side victorious. With the help of his faith, family, and friends, Derek managed to overcome his addiction and find stability. Today, he's doing incredibly well for himself, and we often cross paths at youth meetings. The irony? Ryan and Derek have developed a healthy friendship, and when we meet, it's as if the past was a distant lesson that shaped us all. God truly turned what was once a mess into a message.

It's one of those beautiful, unexpected outcomes that makes you realise how unpredictable life is—and how incredible God's timing can be.

Now, years later, Derek is a testament to God's grace, Ryan is my partner in all things, and I'm finally in a place where I understand the delicate balance between giving and protecting my heart. Relationships aren't about saving someone or being saved – they're about growth, mutual respect, and love, all while maintaining the boundaries that keep you whole.

Looking back on my twenties, I realise that every friendship, every relationship, and every heartbreak was preparing me for the life I have now. I learned how to set boundaries, how to love unconditionally, and most importantly, how to love myself.

I wouldn't trade any of those experiences for the world. Because, as messy and complicated as it all was, it led me to the beautiful life I live today—one filled with love, peace, and the grace of knowing that, with God, even the hardest battles can be won.

A Note from Present Me to the 20-Year-Old Me

Dear 20-Year-Old Me,

You're standing at the threshold of a whirlwind of emotions, aren't you? Love, friendships, family dynamics—each one is pulling you in a different direction, leaving you feeling both exhilarated and exhausted. I know you're trying to navigate it all, and you're making decisions that seem right at the moment, but I want to share a little wisdom from the future that might help you along the way.

First, let's talk about love. You're jumping into relationships with your heart wide open, wearing it on your sleeve for anyone who shows you the slightest bit of attention. It's beautiful that you love so freely, but be careful. Not everyone who catches your eye is meant to hold your heart. You'll learn this the hard way, especially when you find yourself tangled in love triangles, juggling two relationships at once, and losing sight of what you truly want. One of those relationships will cost you a dear friend—someone who has been by your side for years but whom you'll take for granted. It will hurt, and you'll regret it, but it's a lesson that will teach you about the importance of honesty and self-awareness in relationships.

Friendships, too, will be a tricky terrain. You'll find that as you grow and change, not everyone will come along for the ride. Some friendships will fade, and others will end in ways you never expected. But remember this: it's okay. People come into your life for a reason, a season, or a lifetime. The ones who are meant to stay will respect the changes in you, even if they don't fully understand them at first. You'll find a few solid friends who will become your anchors, supporting you through your ups and downs. Cherish them.

Your relationship with your family will be put to the test, especially when it comes to your faith and your choice of a partner. You'll be caught between wanting to be true to yourself and wanting to meet their expectations. It won't be easy. You'll keep secrets, hide your relationship, and hope that one day they'll understand. But when everything comes to light, it won't go as you imagined. There will be anger, disappointment, and a lot of heartache. You'll feel like the black sheep, and your relationship with your parents and brother will be strained. But don't lose hope. Over time, things will change, and so will their understanding of you.

In all of this, boundaries will become your saving grace. You'll learn the hard way that setting boundaries isn't about keeping people out, but about protecting your peace and well-being. Whether it's in friendships, romantic relationships, or family dynamics, knowing where to draw the line will save you from a lot of unnecessary pain. It will also teach you about self-respect and the kind of love you deserve.

So, 20-something-year-old me, take a deep breath. I know you're trying to figure it all out, and it feels overwhelming. But trust me, you'll get through it. You'll make mistakes, you'll learn, and you'll grow. The heartaches, the breakups, the family arguments—they're all part of the journey that will lead you to a place of greater understanding and peace. And remember, no matter what happens, keep your faith close. It will guide you when everything else feels uncertain.

With all my love and understanding,

Your Future Self.

Chapter 4

Career Conundrum: Navigating Career Choices, Finding Financial Independence and Overcoming Obstacles

Chasing her dreams, she stumbled through doubt,
Career paths and choices, a never-ending bout.
In quest for success, financial freedom she sought,
Learning the hard way, lessons were taught.
With every setback, she faced the unknown,
Building her future from the seeds she'd sown.
Through trials and triumphs, her courage is displayed,
A vision of independence, finally unafraid.

The Maze of Career Choices

Navigating the world of careers felt a lot like being dropped into a maze with no map and plenty of dead ends. It was a time filled with both excitement and dread, where each step forward was met with uncertainty about where it would lead. My journey through various career choices began with a lot of trial and error, starting with the Company Secretary course. I thought, "Hey, being a company's secret keeper sounds mysterious and important," but I soon realised it involved more legal jargon and paperwork than I had anticipated. My enthusiasm quickly waned, and I decided to move on.

Next, I found myself in the world of B. Com, thinking that maybe Commerce would be more up my alley. However, as I struggled through balance sheets, financial statements, and the ever-elusive concept of debits and credits, I began to feel like I was swimming in a sea of numbers without a lifeline. Law seemed like the next logical step—after all, I had a knack for arguing, and surely that would translate into a successful legal career, right? But the thought of spending years immersed in endless statutes and case law made me reconsider.

Just when I thought I'd exhausted all my options, my father stepped in with his own suggestion—or rather, his firm decision. "You're doing an MBA," he declared, leaving no room for debate. He believed it would open doors for me, secure my future, and give me the stability I needed. So, off I went, signing up for an MBA course and bracing myself for two more years of sleepless nights, case studies, and group projects that always seemed to require more caffeine than my body could handle.

Discovering My Passion

It wasn't until my last semester of the MBA that I finally began to see the light. Amidst all the chaos and confusion,

I discovered that I had a natural affinity for people. I was fascinated by what made them tick, what motivated them, and how they interacted with one another. It was like a switch had flipped, and I suddenly knew what I wanted to do with my life—Human Resources. I could help people, understand them, and maybe even make a difference in their professional lives. It felt like I'd finally found my calling.

Just as I was coming to this realisation, a job offer landed in my lap from a globally reputed organisation. It was like the universe was finally throwing me a bone, and I wasn't about to let it go to waste. But, as life would have it, things weren't as straightforward as they seemed. I was still reeling from a painful breakup, the kind that leaves you feeling like you've just been hit by a train. To cope, I did what I always did—I threw myself into my work. Work became my refuge, my distraction, my way of numbing the emotional pain that still lingered.

Tasting Financial Freedom: Parties, Shopping Sprees, and Trips Abroad

This was also the time when I finally tasted the sweet freedom of financial independence. From the moment I started earning my own money, I made a vow never to ask my parents for a single rupee again. I saved, I spent, and I indulged in all the things I'd always wanted but never had the means to get. I threw myself into enjoying life to the fullest. Meher and I became partners in crime, hitting up every restaurant that had recently opened, going on wild shopping sprees, and hiding our impulsive buys at each other's houses or in the backseat of my car, and taking fun trips that created memories to last a lifetime.

One of the highlights of this period was my first international trip with Meher—to Uzbekistan, of all places. It was an adventure I hadn't anticipated but one that I thoroughly enjoyed (more so because it wasn't just my first international trip, but one that I was wholly financing myself).

We visited Tashkent, Samarkand, Khiva, and Bukhara over ten unforgettable days. We explored stunning monuments, dined in charming restaurants, shopped in bustling local markets, and revelled in the thrill of playing in the snow at -4 degrees. The authentic Uzbeki food was a delight, and the entire trip was nothing short of splendid.

This working girl experience was eye-opening, and it came with its fair share of work-related perks, including some pretty wild parties. Of course, this was also when I began to experiment with alcohol, using it as another way to numb the pain of my breakup. And, like any self-respecting person with a broken heart and a phone, I made a few drunken calls to Derek. Because, honestly, what's the point of being drunk if you can't remind your ex of your existence at 2 am?

The Corporate Jurassic Park: Surviving the Early Days

Entering the corporate world as a fresh recruit was like walking into Jurassic Park. I quickly realised that it wasn't a walk in the park but more like running from one dinosaur to another. Fortunately, I had an excellent boss who became my mentor. He taught me everything I needed to know, and under his guidance, I soon became one of the top performers. My office became my second home, and I buried myself in work. Looking back, I see that this was another mistake. I was so caught up in proving myself that I forgot to maintain a balance.

Working Long Hours: The Toll of No Work-Life Balance

As I plunged deeper into my career, the lines between work and personal life blurred until they vanished entirely. My days started early and ended late, with little room for anything other than work. I became a fixture at my desk, often working well into the night. The constant pressure to perform and meet deadlines left me with no time to catch my breath, let alone maintain any semblance of work-life balance.

With my work consuming every waking hour, I found myself neglecting other aspects of my life. Exercise, which was once a regular part of my routine, became a distant memory. My daily schedule left no room for any form of physical activity. Weekends, which should have been a time for relaxation and self-care, became an extension of my workweek. I was caught in a relentless cycle of long hours and increasing expectations.

The Physical Toll: Neglecting My Health

It wasn't long before the consequences of my neglect started to manifest physically. Sitting at a desk for hours on end began to take a severe toll on my body. What started as a minor discomfort in my neck gradually escalated into intense pain that refused to go away. Eventually, the pain became so unbearable that I had no choice but to consult a doctor. The diagnosis was a wake-up call: the constant sitting and poor posture had altered the curvature of my spine. The doctor informed me that the lack of movement and proper care had led to significant damage, and I was now paying the price.

For months, I was forced to wear a neck collar to support my spine. The pain was relentless, a constant reminder of how much I had pushed my body to its limits. Despite the doctor's orders to rest and take care of myself, the pressure at work was so overwhelming that I continued to neglect my health. I convinced myself that I didn't have the time to exercise, that the deadlines were more important than my well-being. I was so caught up in the grind that I failed to recognise the long-term consequences of my actions.

The Nightmare: A Brush with Termination

Just when I thought I had life all figured out, a nightmare unfolded. I was recruiting candidates at an agency when one of the coordinators impersonated a candidate during an assessment. My only fault was not being vigilant enough. I was too focused on finishing my work and heading home to notice the deception happening right under my nose. A few weeks later, my boss called me in to discuss the incident. This was a matter of integrity, and the case escalated to the legal team for investigation.

The news spread quickly, not just within our organisation but across the industry. My life, which seemed to be on track, was suddenly derailed by the fear of being fired. I went through multiple rounds of investigation and was even accused of taking bribes. The humiliation was unbearable.

The Mental Toll: A Descent into Darkness

As the investigation into the recruitment incident intensified, so did the strain on my mental health. What had started as a challenging situation quickly spiralled into a nightmare that consumed every aspect of my life. The constant fear of losing my job, coupled with the humiliation of being accused of something I hadn't done, weighed heavily on my mind. I became a shadow of myself, perpetually anxious and terrified of what each new day might bring.

Depression began to creep in, taking root in the corners of my mind. I was constantly worried, unable to shake the gnawing fear that everything I had worked so hard for would be ripped away from me. My thoughts became a relentless loop of self-doubt and dread. What if I never found another job? What if everyone believed the worst about me? What if I really was to blame, even though I couldn't pinpoint where I had gone wrong?

The pressure was unbearable, and it manifested in the worst ways. I would often find myself retreating to the office restroom, where I'd break down in tears, sobbing uncontrollably as the weight of it all became too much to bear. These hysterical breakdowns were my only release, a momentary escape from the crushing reality I faced every day. But they were also deeply humiliating. I felt exposed, vulnerable, and weak – emotions I had never associated with myself before.

People at work began to judge me, their eyes filled with suspicion and disdain. Whispers followed me down the hallways, and I could feel the shift in how I was perceived. It was as if I had become an outcast, someone to be pitied or avoided. The worst part was that this judgement was based on barely any fault of my own. I was caught in a situation that had spun out of control, yet I was the one bearing the brunt of the consequences.

A Crisis of Faith: Questioning God's Plan

Amidst this turmoil, my faith in God – something that had been a cornerstone of my life – began to waver. I found myself questioning Him, crying out in the dead of night, asking why He was allowing me to go through this. What had I done to deserve such suffering? I pleaded for answers, for some understanding of what He was trying to teach me through this ordeal. But the answers didn't come, at least not in the way I wanted them to. Instead, there was only silence, and in that silence, my doubts grew louder.

Every night, I would pray with a heart full of anguish, hoping for some sign, some reassurance that everything would be okay. But all I felt was the overwhelming burden of my circumstances. It felt as though God had abandoned me when I needed Him the most. The faith that had once been my anchor now felt fragile, like it could break at any moment under the weight of my despair.

This crisis of faith was perhaps the hardest part of the entire experience. I had always believed that with God by my side, I could overcome any obstacle. But now, faced with the possibility of losing everything, I began to doubt that belief. I questioned His plan, His timing, and even His presence in my life. The sense of isolation was profound. Not only was I fighting a battle at work, but I was also grappling with an inner turmoil that left me feeling lost and alone.

The Struggle to Hold On: Seeking Strength in The Storm

Despite the deepening darkness, there was a part of me that refused to let go. Even as I questioned God, I clung to the hope that there was a purpose behind all this pain. I told myself that perhaps this was a test, a way to refine my character and deepen my reliance on Him. But these thoughts provided little comfort during the worst moments.

In those days, I learned the true meaning of resilience. Every day was a struggle to hold on, to not give up in the face of overwhelming adversity. My mental health was in tatters, but I forced myself to keep going, to show up at work even when all I wanted to do was hide away from the world. I clung to the belief that this storm would pass, even if I couldn't see how or when.

My bosses stood by me like pillars of strength, advising me not to quit, as that would be seen as an admission of guilt. This ordeal stretched on for over a month until the day my boss received an email saying I was to be terminated. It felt like the ground had been pulled out from under me.

The Turnaround: A Lesson in Resilience and Integrity

Just when I thought all was lost, my boss sent me home with a simple instruction – to trust him. He risked his own job to clear my name, taking a warning letter on my behalf. I was handed a level 3 warning, meaning that for the next six months, I was at risk of losing my job. My chance at a promotion was gone, and every piece of work I submitted was scrutinised.

This period taught me more about myself than I had ever imagined. I discovered a strength I didn't know I possessed – the strength to endure, to keep moving forward even when everything seemed to be falling apart. And slowly, as the days turned into weeks, I began to see the faintest glimmers of hope.

The ordeal wasn't over, and the scars it left would remain with me for a long time. But I emerged from it with a deeper understanding of what it means to trust in God, even when His plan seems inscrutable. I learned that faith isn't just about believing when things are going well; it's about holding on even in the darkest of times, when the path ahead is uncertain, and the ground beneath your feet feels unsteady.

But the biggest lesson I learned through this ordeal was one of resilience and integrity. I never slacked off again. Instead, I slowed down, trod carefully, and learned to trust that with God by my side, nothing truly wrong could happen.

In the end, it was this lesson that stayed with me – a lesson in faith, resilience, and the power of not giving up, even when the odds are stacked against you.

A Note from Present Me to the 20-Year-Old Me

Dear 20-Something-Year-Old Me,

I know you're standing at the edge of a vast, uncertain future, heart pounding with both excitement and fear. You've got dreams that reach the sky and a list of "what-ifs" that's just as long. You're about to dive into the deep end of career choices, financial independence, and all the obstacles that come with them. Trust me, the waters will get rough, and there will be times when you feel like you're drowning. But I'm here to tell you: keep swimming.

First off, it's okay to be confused about what you want to do in life. You'll dabble in a few different fields—Company Secretary, B. Com, Law—and you'll feel the pressure from every side, especially from dad, who just wants the best for you but doesn't always understand your dreams. Eventually, you'll find your calling in Human Resources during your MBA. It'll click, and you'll realise that you're a people person through and through. You'll find joy in helping others find their place in the world, just as you're finding yours.

Your journey won't be a straight path. You'll make mistakes—big ones—and you'll face challenges that will make you question everything. There will be sleepless nights, days when you feel like the world is against you, and moments when your confidence will be shaken to its core. But remember, these are the moments that will shape you into who you're meant to be. Each obstacle is a lesson in disguise, each setback a stepping stone to something greater.

You'll also experience the thrill of financial independence. The first time you earn your own money, it'll feel like a rush of freedom unlike anything else. You'll learn to manage your finances, make your own decisions, and discover the joy of spending on things that make you happy—like that first international trip to Uzbekistan. Savour these moments because they'll remind you that you're capable of standing on your own two feet.

But with independence comes responsibility. Working long hours will take a toll on you, and you'll learn the hard way that work-life balance isn't just a buzzword—it's a necessity. You'll neglect your health, and it will catch up with you. So please, take care of yourself. Exercise, eat well, and make time for things that bring you joy outside of work. Your body and mind will thank you later.

And then there's that dark time—when everything seems to crumble around you, and you'll face the possibility of losing it all. You'll question your abilities, your choices, even your faith in God. You'll cry, you'll break down, and you'll wonder if you'll ever make it through. But listen to me: you will. You'll emerge from that storm stronger, wiser, and with a deeper understanding of what it means to have integrity and resilience. The lessons you learn during this time will be some of the most important ones of your life.

So, 20-Something-Year-Old Me, take a deep breath. You're about to embark on an incredible journey. It won't be easy, and there will be times when you'll want to give up. But don't. Keep pushing forward because the person you're going to become is someone you'll be proud of. Trust yourself, lean on God, and remember that every twist and turn is part of the adventure.

With all my love and wisdom,

Your Future Self.

Chapter 5

The Grace of Surrender: Accepting What Is

In surrender's embrace, she faced the deep,
Learning that control's a fickle keep.
Through trials of faith, her spirit aligned,
Finding peace in letting go, a heart refined.
Amidst the chaos, she learned to trust,
To accept the flow, as she must.
In the grace of surrender, strength was found,
A new path emerged, her feet on solid ground.

The Witch Hunt: Two Years Later and Still No Groom

Let me set the scene for you: it had been two years since my breakup with Derek, and my parents were treating my single status as if it were a crisis on par with a national disaster. In the world of Indian households, being a single woman in your late twenties is akin to committing a crime against society. My parents, who had once been content with a casual inquiry here or there about potential suitors, had now turned into full-time detectives in the great husband hunt.

"Khushie, don't you think it's time to get serious about settling down?" became the background music of my life, with my mom and dad taking turns playing the DJ. Every family gathering, every festival, every time the phone rang, I braced myself for the inevitable question: "So, any news on the marriage front?"

But I wasn't exactly sitting idly by either. After all, I did go on several dates, met a few guys through family connections, and even tried to convince myself that maybe, just maybe, one of them would click. Spoiler alert: none of them did. It wasn't that these guys were terrible (though a few were, let's be honest), but I just couldn't shake the feeling that something was missing.

And that something was Derek. Somewhere deep down, I was still holding onto the hope that we would somehow find our way back to each other. But with each passing day, it became clearer that God had other plans.

Matrimony Madness: The Circus of Mismatches

Then came the pandemic—cue ominous music—and the great matrimonial madness of 2020. While most people were busy learning to bake bread or binge-watching *Ozark*, my father took it upon himself to turn our living room into Matrimony Central.

My profile was up on every matrimony site you could think of, and the proposals started rolling in at an alarming rate. I kid you not; I was receiving 40-50 profiles a day. If I thought finding the right guy was hard before, this was like trying to find a needle in a haystack where most of the hay was, well, just hay.

Now, my father, God bless him, had the filtering skills of a goldfish. "He seems nice," he would say, showing me a profile of a guy who was 10 years older, lived in a village I couldn't pronounce, and had a passion for tailoring (nothing against tailoring, but come on). "Dad, I'm looking for someone who's at least taller than me and, you know, not already eligible for a senior citizen discount."

But it didn't stop there. For every profile I rejected, my father demanded a detailed analysis. "Why not this one? He's a doctor!" Sure, Dad, but he's also 5'2", and I'm pretty sure he looks like he could be my uncle. "Your criteria are too unrealistic," he'd huff. "You're not giving these guys a chance."

I started to feel like Goldilocks, but instead of finding the porridge that was just right, all I got was a series of mismatched suitors. Too short, too old, too boring, too remote, too… well, just not right.

Let's talk about some of the characters who came my way. There was the guy who, after one conversation, sent me a ten-page document outlining his expectations from a wife, complete with footnotes and references (true story). Then there was the dude who ghosted me after I casually mentioned I liked dogs. Apparently, he was more of a cat person—okay, buddy, whatever helps you sleep at night.

The whole process was like a bad episode of The Bachelor, except I wasn't handing out roses, and there wasn't any dramatic music to make things seem more exciting. Instead, there was just my dad's ever-growing Excel sheet of potential suitors and my mom's constant reminders that I wasn't getting any younger.

The Moment of Surrender: A Shower Revelation

After months of this matrimonial madness, I was hanging by a thread. The constant stream of mismatches, the pressure from my parents, and the lingering hope that maybe, just maybe, Derek and I could still work things out—it was all too much. I was spiralling into frustration and despair.

Then came January 1st, 2021. I remember the day vividly because it was the day I hit rock bottom, which, as it turns out, was also the day I found my way back up. I was in the bath, trying to soak away the stress, when it hit me like a ton of bricks. I started crying, not just a few tears, but full-on ugly crying—the kind where your face contorts, and you make sounds that are anything but dignified.

I let out everything I had been holding in. The frustration, the heartbreak, the disappointment—it all came pouring out. I threw my hands up in the air (well, as much as you can throw your hands up in a shower without splashing water everywhere) and cried out to God. "I surrender, God! I'm done trying to control this. I don't want to hold onto Derek anymore. I need You to take over. I need You to find me the right man that You have in store for me. I'm letting go."

And just like that, in the middle of my meltdown, I felt a wave of calm wash over me. It was as if all the tension I had been carrying around for months melted away with the bathwater. For the first time in what felt like forever, I felt at peace. I knew that I had to stop trying to force things to happen and just trust that whatever was meant to be would be.

A few days later, I talked to my mentor about what had happened. I asked him, with more than a hint of doubt in my voice, "How am I ever going to find someone who will understand and respect me for who I am?" His response was simple, but it struck a chord. "You'll be surprised how God will use your messy situation. You may find your perfect match here."

And so, with a newfound sense of calm and a heart full of hope, I decided to let go and let God take the lead. Little did I know that my perfect match was just around the corner—literally.

The Arrival of Ryan: Tall, Handsome, And Everything I Asked For

Enter Ryan. It was February 15th, 2021, and my phone buzzed with a new message. I glanced at it and saw Ryan's name. It wasn't a grand romantic gesture or a dramatic love letter – it was just a simple text introducing himself. But for me, it was the beginning of something that felt like it might actually be worth holding onto.

Let me describe Ryan for you because, well, he deserves a proper introduction. Ryan was 6'3" tall, with a fair complexion and the kind of looks that make people do a double take. You know, the kind of guy you see in movies and think, "Yeah, that doesn't happen in real life." Except it did, and I was now texting with him.

We exchanged messages for a few days, and there was an instant connection. He was funny, charming, and best of all, he seemed genuinely interested in getting to know me. I found myself surprisingly at ease. We talked about everything under the sun—our favourite movies, music, and of course, our bizarre dating experiences. It felt refreshingly normal, and I began to hope that maybe, just maybe, this one could be different. But, of course, I wasn't going to let my parents in on this just yet. I wanted to meet him on my own terms, without any family interference. So, I told my parents I had to go into the office on Saturday, when in reality, I was gearing up for a date that could either be the start of something amazing or yet another full stop. I told them I was going to work, which wasn't entirely a lie; my work was just going to be meeting a potential suitor instead of spreadsheets. I wore a beige floral top, blue jeans and sneakers, slapped on a little makeup, not too much since I had to go undercover, and dressed in my favourite yet understated outfit—something that said, "I've got this," but didn't scream "I'm trying too hard."

The First Date: Dramatic Entrance, Nervous Heartbeats, and Chivalry

I drove to the mall, my mind buzzing with a million thoughts. My car was parked strategically close to the entrance, allowing me to make a dramatic entrance, should things go south (or simply to make sure I had a quick escape route). As I entered the mall, in a moment of rebellious independence, I decided to do a bit of impromptu shopping. I didn't really need anything, but I figured it would be a good way to kill time and keep my mind off the impending encounter. I wanted Ryan to be the one waiting, not the other way around. I saw Ryan's silver Creta waiting at the entrance. My heart skipped a beat as I spotted him in the driver's seat.

But let's rewind a bit. The plan was to meet at the mall and then head to a restaurant for lunch. As I reached the entrance, I got a call from Ryan. His voice, smooth and reassuring, did nothing to calm my nerves but made me even more anxious. "Hey Khushie, I'm here, waiting for you in the silver Creta."

I replied with my best attempt at nonchalance, "Be right there," and hung up. As I walked towards his car, I couldn't help but mentally run through my checklist: Is he tall enough? Does he have a sense of humour? Is he as handsome as his pictures?

When I reached the car, he got out to open the door for me. I couldn't help but notice his impeccable sense of style: a black t-shirt, a stylish jacket, dark blue jeans, and sleek black Adidas shoes. And, of course, he was wearing a mask—thanks, COVID—so our initial interaction was a masked mystery.

We exchanged a rather awkward hug—one of those where you're not quite sure if you should go for a handshake or a full embrace. "Nice to meet you," I said, trying not to blush. "Yeah, nice to meet you too," Ryan replied with a charming smile.

As we drove to the restaurant, a good 40 minutes away, we kept our masks on and communicated mainly through eye contact. And let me tell you, his eyes were like liquid caramel, glowing softly in the sunlight. I was having a hard time concentrating on the conversation because I was too busy mentally checking off the boxes on my list: tall—check, handsome—check, respectful—double check.

During the drive, we talked about everything from our families to our favourite movies, and even the kinds of music we enjoyed. I asked him a crucial question: Why was he looking to get married so young? His answer surprised me more than I expected. He shared that he had been in a long-term relationship with someone from a different religion, and when her family didn't approve, they broke up. Since then, he had been searching for someone who was right for him, and he had made a pact with himself that the next person he met should be "the one", or he would stop looking.

I was floored. Here was a guy who not only understood the complexities of relationships but also didn't care much about religious boundaries. He respected individuality and seemed genuinely open-minded. My heart was doing a little happy dance, but I was still wary. All my past experiences had taught me to wait and see.

The Connection: Effortless and Refreshing

Arriving at the restaurant, we finally took off our masks. The ease and comfort we felt with each other were surprising. We had connected so well despite only seeing each other's eyes for most of the drive. Our conversation flowed effortlessly. For the first time in a long while, I felt genuinely at ease with someone.

Lunch was an absolute delight. We talked about our expectations from marriage, our hobbies, and even our pet peeves. Ryan was hilarious and had a knack for making me laugh. He cracked the silliest jokes and had me in stitches. We discussed everything from our favourite movies to our mutual dislike of tattoos. Just for fun, I raised my eyebrow and, with a very serious expression, told him I had a tattoo. Ryan was taken aback and asked me three times if I was joking. It was one of the funniest moments of the day.

We shared an ice cream for dessert and continued our conversation. To my surprise, we had both attended the same college for five years. Although he was in the Arts section and I was in Commerce, we never crossed paths. It was an interesting coincidence and another point in the "things that make you go hmmm" column.

We spent eight hours together, and time seemed to fly by. As we hugged goodbye—this time less awkwardly—I couldn't help but reflect on how refreshing and different this experience had been. For the first time in a long while, I felt at ease and hopeful. It was as if God was finally showing me a glimpse of what I had been waiting for.

The Beginning of Something New: Hope and Caution

After the first date, I was on cloud nine but also on high alert. I made notes, analysed every detail, and kept myself guarded, though I couldn't help but feel that this might be the start of something special. Ryan seemed to tick all the boxes, but I had learned not to take anything for granted. I felt a mix of emotions. It was as if time had flown by in a blink. We decided to meet again the following weekend, and I went home, replaying every moment of the day in my mind. I found myself analysing every detail—every word, every glance, every joke. I was overwhelmed but not in a bad way. It was more like I was trying to process the fact that everything seemed to be aligning perfectly.

I was still on guard, though. I kept thinking, "How can someone be this perfect? There has to be a catch." But for the moment, I decided to hold onto the hope that maybe, just maybe, Ryan was everything I had been waiting for. My mind was a whirlwind of thoughts: Was he truly interested? Would this be the start of a new chapter? I even started crafting a mental list of things I wanted to discuss on our next date. The scepticism I felt wasn't about him but rather about my own tendency to overthink everything.

The Follow-Up: Dates 2, 3, and Beyond

As the weeks went by, Ryan and I continued to meet, and each date seemed better than the last. We explored new restaurants, took long walks, and had deep conversations. With every interaction, I found myself more and more drawn to him. The initial excitement transformed into something deeper, something that felt right.

During this time, I began to share more about my past, my insecurities, and my journey. Ryan listened with genuine interest and empathy. He never judged me for my past relationships or my struggles; instead, he embraced me with all my flaws. It was a stark contrast to some of the other suitors I had met, who seemed more interested in ticking off boxes on a checklist than in understanding who I truly was. Ryan and I continued to see each other; each encounter revealing more layers of his personality and deepening my feelings for him. We navigated the challenges of dating during a pandemic, from virtual calls to socially distanced walks, with a sense of humour and mutual respect.

I eventually introduced Ryan to my family; his genuine nature and respect for our traditions won them over. It was a journey of letting go of old expectations and embracing new possibilities, all while holding onto the faith that had guided me through the ups and downs of my search for the right partner.

The First Family Visit: Nervous Anticipation, A Chirpy Surprise, and Meeting the Clan

After a few dates with Ryan, things were getting serious. This was no longer just casual dinner and movie nights. The day arrived when I would finally meet his family—a pivotal moment that sent my anxiety levels through the roof. It wasn't just about making a good first impression; it was about answering a million questions swirling in my mind. My palms were sweating, my heart raced, and I couldn't stop fidgeting with my jumpsuit. I'd picked it out days in advance, yet at that moment, I couldn't help but wonder if it screamed, "she's trying too hard." Would they like me? Was I dressed appropriately? Would I be able to adjust to living in a joint family? And the biggest question of all—would they accept a girl who couldn't cook for herself, let alone for six people?

As someone who was used to living under the watchful eye of a conservative family, I knew that navigating Ryan's joint family would be no cakewalk. The very thought of his grandparents scrutinising me made my palms sweat. I couldn't help but imagine his grandmother pointing a bony finger at me and saying, "She doesn't even know how to cook a proper meal!" The horror!

Ryan, ever the gentleman, knew I was anxious and decided to come pick me up. The drive to his place was filled with my endless questions. "What if they don't like me?" I fretted. "What if I don't fit in?" Ryan, as calm as ever, simply chuckled and reassured me, "You'll be fine, Khushie. Just be yourself." Easy for him to say—he wasn't the one meeting a potential lifetime of in-laws! It wasn't like we hadn't discussed marriage before, but meeting the family meant things were real. Like, really real.

As we approached his society, my heart was racing. The trees lining the driveway seemed to mock me with their serenity, swaying gently in the breeze, as if they had no idea of the impending doom I felt. We parked the car, and as I was mentally preparing myself for a battle, the car door flung open, and a tiny whirlwind in a sleeveless lavender top and dark blue trousers hopped into the backseat. Before I knew what was happening, she wrapped me in a hug and said, "Hi, I'm Behzad! Oh my God, I'm so excited to meet you!"

I couldn't quite process how someone so tiny could exude so much energy. She was stunning too, with a glowing smile that seemed to instantly melt away a layer of my anxiety. I didn't even get a chance to introduce myself before she started chatting about how great it was that we were going to lunch together. "Behzad" was Ryan's mom, though calling her "mom" didn't seem right for someone who looked more like his stylish older sister.

Behzad - who I immediately started calling "Mommy B" in my head - was exactly the type of person who could become your best friend within five minutes. She wasn't just beautiful; she was the kind of person who radiates warmth - like hot chocolate on a cold day.

The Lunch that Could Have Been a Soap Opera

By the time we arrived at the hotel, I was no longer a ball of nerves. Behzad—or *Mommy B,* as I later started calling her—had worked her magic on me. As we waited for Ryan to park the car, she wrapped her hand around mine, fingers interlinked, and whispered, "I love your jumpsuit, but you should wear whatever you feel like. Before I got married, I dressed just like this, and you know what my mother-in-law told me? 'Have it, flaunt it.'" She winked. At that moment, I knew she and I were going to get along *very* well.

As we sat for lunch, Mommy B and I bonded over Ryan's hilariously awkward dating experiences and the circus that is the matrimonial search. I soon realised that Behzad wasn't just Ryan's mom—she was his friend, his confidante, and an absolute riot. She was outspoken, bold, and had a brilliant career. She was both a life coach and a businesswoman, an impressive combination of smarts and sass. Like me, she too came from a strict background but had transformed after marriage into the woman she was meant to be. It was like seeing a future version of myself, and suddenly, I wasn't as nervous anymore. With Mommy B around, I knew that acceptance, love, and encouragement would always be a part of my life.

The House of Giggles and Tea

After lunch, we headed back to Ryan's house, where I met his cheerful, fun-loving father. He cracked jokes and made me feel at ease, instantly making me laugh with his light-hearted humour. Then came the grandparents—a meeting I had been dreading for weeks. But to my surprise, his grandfather reminded me so much of my own late grandad, and his grandmother was just as friendly, full of light-hearted jokes that made the atmosphere even more relaxed. The entire family dynamic was one of joy, laughter, and mutual respect. I could breathe again.

As Ryan dropped me home that evening, I knew I would be just fine in this family. They were a cheerful, supportive bunch, and most importantly, I felt welcomed. I also knew, without a doubt, that I wanted to marry Ryan—no matter how difficult the struggles might be.

The Quirks of Love: Ryan's OCD Battle

But let's not sugarcoat things. Ryan came with his own set of quirks. His biggest battle was with Obsessive-Compulsive Disorder (OCD), and it wasn't your run-of-the-mill "I like things tidy" kind of OCD. No, Ryan loved fiercely—almost too much—which manifested as an overbearing desire to protect and care for his loved ones. He cared so much that it became obsessive. He wanted to know what I ate, how much I exercised, and if I was living "healthily"—the list went on.

Now, coming from a family where freedom was something I had to fight tooth and nail for, I wasn't exactly thrilled at the thought of jumping from one set of restrictions into another. Let's just say, I wasn't exactly thrilled.

We had our share of fights and arguments, and while I gave him a pushback at times, there were moments when I gave in too. It was hard—no, *really* hard.

No one is perfect, and Ryan was on his own journey of healing. I believed that God had placed me in his life for a reason—that I had the strength to help him overcome his struggles. I saw the future Ryan, free from his OCD, and that potential kept me going. I knew that our relationship would require patience, understanding, and a whole lot of love.

Ryan's struggles terrified him, but they also gave him purpose. My presence in his life gave him a reason to change, to live without being so stressed and fearful all the time. I prayed daily for the strength to cope and to deal with him in the gentlest way possible. Oddly enough, this journey taught me to *listen*, a skill that had never been my strong suit, but it became a necessity.

The Terrace Talk That Changed Everything

One day, his mom—sweet, vibrant Mommy B—noticed that the stress of dealing with Ryan's issues was weighing on me. She took me to the terrace while it was pouring rain, and we sat under the shade. "If you decide not to marry Ryan," she said softly, "I will support you. If you ever think of leaving him, I won't stand in your way. You are the daughter I've always longed for, and I will love you just as much as I love him."

Her words were like a lifeline. Here was this incredible woman, telling me it was okay to walk away if I needed to, even though she clearly adored her son. I was in awe of her, especially coming from my mother-in-law even before I was officially married. But I wasn't one to leave when things got tough. I loved Ryan, quirks and all, and I knew I could help him through his journey. I was committed to standing by him, no matter what challenges we faced. If anything, his mother's words strengthened my resolve.

The Unconventional Family Meeting: A Vaccination Affair

In a twist of fate that could only happen in the age of COVID, our families met for the first time at a vaccination centre. Yes, you read that right. While most couples have their families meet over a nice dinner or a cosy gathering at home, we had ours meet while getting vaccinated together. It was, in a word, hilarious.

There we were, all lined up like soldiers waiting for our shots, trying to make small talk while the nurses prepped the vaccines. My father, who had been eager to meet Ryan's family ever since he got to know about Ryan and my relationship, found the whole situation absurdly amusing. He kept cracking jokes about how the vaccine would now seal the deal between our families. Meanwhile, my mother, who had always been supportive of my relationship with Ryan, was all smiles, thrilled that everything was finally coming together—albeit in the most unconventional way.

Ryan's family was equally amused. His father, ever the joker, made light of the situation, while his mother, Mommy B, looked at my mom with that knowing smile, as if to say, "This is just the beginning of our crazy family adventures."

Here we were, about to embark on one of life's most important meetings, and instead of a fancy dinner or traditional family gathering, we were all rolling up our sleeves for vaccines. Classic.

A Blossoming Relationship: Weekends, Walks, and Nosy Neighbours

As the months passed, our relationship continued to blossom. I spent my weekends at Ryan's place, arriving in the morning and staying until after dinner. Ryan, ever the dedicated partner, tagged along with his laptop and worked from my home during the weekdays. We enjoyed our lunches together, took walks in my extremely nosy society—where all the neighbours seemed to poke their heads out to get a glimpse of the tall, handsome boy I was walking with—and grew closer to each other's families. I could practically hear the neighbours gossiping about the tall, handsome boy I was walking with. Honestly, it was like being in a soap opera, complete with the side-eye stares and head turns.

My father, still recovering from my rebellious streak, would often tell me that I was lucky to have met a boy like Ryan. He'd remind me to behave myself and not mess things up, adding that Ryan's family was influential, and I wouldn't find better. It was his way of expressing concern, subtle, right? Though it was clear that he had started to warm up to Ryan.

My mother, on the other hand, couldn't be happier. She laughed and teased me about how I had a long list of high standards, but the moment I met Ryan, I melted like butter on a warm pan. She loved how Ryan made me laugh and was overjoyed that I had finally found the love I deserved.

The Best Friend Meets the Boyfriend: A Nerve-Wracking Lunch

For months, Meher had been privy to all the details about my relationship with Ryan—the dates, the sweet gestures, and even our meeting with his family. She was my sounding board, the one who celebrated every milestone in my life. Ryan, too, knew about Meher. I made sure he understood just how important she was to me, how much a part of my life she had always been. It was crucial for me that these two pivotal people in my life got along.

Then came the day when the inevitable had to happen—Meher, Ryan, and I were finally going to meet. I was a bundle of nerves. My mind raced with a million what-ifs: What if they didn't like each other? What if they didn't click? What if my friendship with Meher changed after I got married? Would she feel sidelined? After all, like they say in Hindi, "Shaadi ke baad sab badal jaata hai" (Everything changes after marriage). These fears swirled around in my head as we approached the lunch.

As we sat down to eat, the tension in my stomach was unbearable, but to my immense relief, the moment Meher's infectious laugh broke the ice, the nerves began to settle. The conversation flowed naturally. Ryan, with his charming and easy-going personality, meshed with Meher's giddy-headed energy. They bantered, they laughed, and for the first time, I exhaled.

It wasn't just that they got along, though. In no time, Meher became a regular fixture at Ryan's house. Weekends were filled with spontaneous trips to hill stations, where we'd spend the day laughing, exploring, and eating our way through mountain cafés. We'd frequent new restaurants together, creating a little trio of adventure. What was even more surprising was how Ryan and Meher's bond evolved. They went from strangers to something closer to siblings. They teased each other relentlessly, fought over silly things, but also trusted each other deeply.

This was my biggest fear, now removed entirely. My best friend hadn't been lost in my new chapter of marriage – if anything, she was more a part of my life than ever. And even better? Ryan had gained a best friend too.

The Big Proposal

It was a lazy Sunday afternoon, and everything felt cosy. Ryan and I were snuggled up in bed watching *Blood and Bone*, one of those action-packed films he loved, while I pretended to be totally engrossed. In reality, I was more excited about the fact that we had the entire day to ourselves. Thanks to a statewide lockdown, all the shops were closed, and we were free from the usual obligations that had us darting around on weekends. It was just us, enjoying the quiet comfort of each other's company.

Later that day, some family friends were supposed to come over. These were the kind of fancy people for whom you dress up, even if it's a pandemic and no one's really going anywhere special. Mommy B was always one to make a grand occasion out of even the smallest gathering, and today was no different. I could already hear her voice telling me to look my best, which, for her, meant nails done, hair perfectly styled, and an outfit that screamed "ready for a photoshoot."

So, naturally, I was in no rush to move. "Can we just stay in bed?" I asked, secretly hoping she'd forget about the guests and let us keep lounging. But no, Mommy B had other plans—big plans. The kind of plans that would change everything.

"Come on, we should get ready," Ryan nudged me, his usual calm demeanour betraying nothing. I dragged myself out of bed, expecting nothing more than an afternoon of forced small talk and smiles. Little did I know, this day was about to take a very unexpected turn.

We got dressed and headed to Mommy B's room. Ryan entered first, and I followed a few minutes later, still mentally preparing myself for an afternoon of socialising. As soon as I walked in, something felt different. The room was dimly lit, and the scent of roses filled the air. I stopped in my tracks, my eyes widening in surprise. There, stuck to the door, was a single red rose. Rose petals were scattered across the floor, forming a delicate path that led to the bed. And there, right in the centre, was a cake. But not just any cake—this one had "Will You Marry Me?" written on top, with the most beautiful diamond ring sitting right on it.

I froze, my heart racing as I tried to process what was happening. Was this real? Was this *actually* happening? I had seen proposals in movies and on Instagram, but now it was my turn. My proposal. My moment.

Ryan, my calm and collected Ryan, knelt down on one knee, his eyes locked on mine. "Will you marry me?" he asked, his voice steady yet filled with so much emotion that it made my heart swell.

I didn't even think—I just screamed, "Of course I will!" It was a perfect moment of pure joy, disbelief, and excitement. The ring fit perfectly, like it was always meant to be on my finger. It sparkled under the soft lights, symbolising the start of our forever.

In true Ryan fashion, he didn't make a grand speech or turn it into a drawn-out affair. He simply asked, and I simply said yes, and that was all we needed. It wasn't flashy or extravagant, but it was us. Simple, honest, and real.

After the initial shock wore off, we immediately drove to my parents' house to break the news. I couldn't stop looking at the ring on my hand, still in disbelief that I was officially engaged. The moment we walked in, my mom knew something was up. Her eyes lit up with anticipation, and when I flashed my hand, the excitement in the room exploded. My parents were overjoyed, my brother gave me a bear hug, and for the first time, it really hit me: I was going to marry Ryan. We were going to start a life together.

The Joyful Scream: Sharing the Moment with My Best Friend

The moment Ryan slipped the sparkling ring onto my finger, my first instinct wasn't just to bask in the excitement alone – it was to share the moment with Meher, my best friend and confidante. Without a second thought, I grabbed my phone and video-called her. As soon as she answered, her eyes widened in disbelief, then immediately lit up with excitement.

"I said yes!" I shrieked, showing her the dazzling ring.

In true Meher fashion, she didn't just squeal—she screamed. Loudly. We both did, actually, jumping up and down in pure, unfiltered joy like we were little girls again, caught in a moment of giddiness that no words could quite describe. It was as if all the years of friendship, all the heart-to-heart conversations, and all the dreams we shared had culminated in this one electric, surreal moment.

That evening, Ryan and I met up with Meher to celebrate what had just unfolded. The three of us—our little trio—sat together, smiling until our faces hurt. We clicked pictures, each one capturing the joy, the laughter, and the promise of what was to come.

It wasn't just a celebration of my engagement to Ryan; it was a celebration of the journey Meher and I had been on together, and the beautiful way she had embraced this new chapter of my life.

It was the happiest day of my life so far. I was officially his, and he was mine. Our forever had officially begun.

That proposal marked the end of one chapter of our lives and the start of another. It was a defining moment, not just for us as a couple, but for me as a person. It wasn't just about saying yes to Ryan – it was about saying yes to all the challenges, growth, and joy that would come with our future together.

Embracing The Unexpected

As the excitement of the engagement faded into the rhythm of everyday life, I began to reflect on the journey that had brought me here—both in love and in life. It was not a fairytale, but something far more real. With each twist and turn, I learned some of the most profound lessons that came from surrendering to what is rather than clinging to what I thought should be.

First, I learned the importance of embracing imperfection—both in myself and in others. Ryan wasn't perfect, and neither was I. In fact, I spent so much of my life trying to control my surroundings, avoid mistakes, and navigate life with a fear of failure. But with Ryan, I learned that it's not about finding someone who fits an ideal mould. It's about choosing to love someone through their struggles, seeing their potential, and having faith in the journey you're both on.

Next came the lesson of letting go of expectations. In the beginning, I was filled with preconceived notions about love, relationships, and what it meant to meet someone's family. I had anxieties and fears that turned out to be unfounded. Behzad, with her warmth and wisdom, taught me that sometimes the most liberating thing you can do is to let go of the rigid expectations you set for yourself and others. Life has a funny way of surprising you when you stop trying to control every detail.

Perhaps the most significant lesson was learning the art of patience. Both Ryan and I brought our own baggage to the table, and adjusting to each other's quirks and challenges took time. For me, surrendering meant understanding that healing and growth don't happen overnight. There were times I wanted to fix everything right away, but I had to accept that Ryan's journey with his OCD, much like my own struggles with anxiety, was a long and winding road. Surrendering meant acknowledging that love doesn't mean solving every problem; it means supporting each other through them.

But at the core of this chapter in my life was the lesson of faith. Not just faith in God, but faith in the process of life itself. Surrendering wasn't about giving up, but rather trusting that things would unfold as they were meant to, even when the path ahead wasn't clear. I had to let go of my need for control and lean into the belief that, in the end, everything would work out—even if it didn't look the way I had imagined.

Surrendering also meant learning to accept help, something I'd long struggled with. Whether it was Mommy B offering her unconditional support or Ryan helping me work through my fears, I had to recognise that I didn't have to navigate life alone. Accepting love and guidance from others isn't a sign of weakness; it's an act of grace.

In the end, the grace of surrender wasn't about giving up control – it was about accepting the beauty of what is, rather than wishing for something different. It was about trusting in love, in growth, and in the unfolding of life's unpredictable, often messy, but ultimately beautiful journey.

I realised that, in surrendering, I didn't lose myself – I found a deeper version of me. I discovered strength in my vulnerability, and peace in letting go. Surrender became not just a lesson, but a way of living – one that allowed love to flourish, imperfections and all.

And so, with a heart full of gratitude, I stepped forward into this new chapter of my life, knowing that while I couldn't control what was to come, I could always choose to surrender with grace, trusting that the best was yet to unfold – and it surely did.

A Note from Present Me to 20-Year-Old Me

Dear 20-Something-Year-Old Me,

I know you're feeling lost right now, swimming in a sea of uncertainty, trying to figure out who you are and what your place in this world is. You're dealing with heartache, navigating a strict household, and trying to patch together a sense of independence while still holding on to the expectations of everyone around you. You're confused, overwhelmed, and you feel like you need to have all the answers—but let me tell you a secret: you don't.

*If there's one thing I wish I could whisper to you, it's **breathe**. You don't need to have it all figured out just yet. I know that's hard to accept because you're a planner, a perfectionist, and someone who wants to control every detail of your life. But the truth is, life is going to throw you curveballs that no amount of planning can prevent. And you know what? That's okay.*

*The next few years of your life are going to be full of highs and lows, unexpected twists, and challenges you won't see coming. You're going to meet people who will change you, for better or worse. You'll stumble, fall, and sometimes feel like you're going backward instead of forward. But trust me when I say, **every experience you go through has a purpose**. Even the pain, even the mistakes—especially the mistakes.*

*You'll soon learn that real strength isn't about holding everything together perfectly. It's about **letting go**, accepting things as they are, and finding peace in the messiness of life. I know right now that surrender sounds like giving up to you. But with time, you'll see that surrendering is the bravest thing you can do. It's about trusting that you'll land on your feet even when you don't* *know where the ground is. It's about embracing uncertainty and knowing that you are enough, exactly as you are.*

You'll learn that love, in all its forms—romantic, familial, and even self-love—requires patience and grace. Not just for others, but for yourself. The people you meet along the way will teach you lessons that no book or degree could. Some will test you, push your buttons, and challenge the way you see the world. Others will fill your heart with so much joy that you'll wonder how you ever lived without them. But all of them will help shape you into the person you are meant to become.

So, 20-Something-Year-Old Me, I want you to know this: **you don't have to have it all figured out**. *Be kind to yourself. Give yourself permission to make mistakes, to take risks, to say "no" to the things that don't feel right and "yes" to the things that set your soul on fire. Don't be afraid to let go of the need for control and surrender to the flow of life. Trust me, some of the best things that will ever happen to you will be the things you didn't plan.*

Lastly, remember this: **you are so much stronger than you know**. *You'll face battles you never expected, and you'll come out the other side with a heart that is braver, softer, and more open. So, hold your head high, take a deep breath, and know that everything you're going through right now is just the beginning of a beautiful, imperfect journey.*

With all my love and encouragement,

Your Future Self

P.S. You're going to be okay. Better than okay, actually. You're going to thrive.

Chapter 6

The Vow-Factor: The Endless Dance Between Chaos and Order

In the shadows of doubt, her faith took flight,
Navigating the storm, she sought the light.
With a heart open wide and hope on the mend,
She learned that in change, old wounds could bend.
From loss and love, she found her way,
Embracing the pain, she began to sway.
In each trial, a lesson, a chance to renew,
She discovered the strength in her heart so true.

Love, Road Trips, And the Proposal of "Sleepovers"

Now that Ryan and I were officially engaged, we were getting closer, fonder, and more inseparable than ever. We did all the fun couple things—road trips, spontaneous photo shoots, and binge-watching action movies that I pretended to love. Our adventures were filled with excitement and loads of laughter. I lost count of how many pictures we took. I am the type of girl who'd stop the car just to capture the "perfect sunset," while he mostly rolled his eyes and tried to strike a pose that said, "I'm effortlessly beautiful, not posing for Instagram."

But despite all this, there was something more we both wanted, and it wasn't just more photos of sunsets. No, we wanted to spend the *entire* day together. Not just daylight hours, but also nights. Now, let me explain—Ryan's place was practically my second home. I was there for lunch, tea, and sometimes dinner. But when it came to spending the night, oh no, that was forbidden.

Apparently, in my world, it's against all laws of nature for a girl to sleep over before she's officially married. My brother and his fiancée were already practically cohabitating, which only made it worse for me because, of course, there's nothing more unfair than watching your sibling get away with the very thing you're banned from. It's like being told to share a toy, but only your brother is allowed to actually play with it.

So, there we were—me giving my puppy dog eyes to my parents and Ryan brainstorming ways we could sneak around this "no-sleepover" policy without causing World War III. But as luck (or rain, in this case) would have it, one Saturday night, everything changed.

The Rainy Sleepover (Thank You, Mother Nature)

It was a regular post-dinner Saturday, except for the fact that the heavens had opened up, and it was pouring cats, dogs, and possibly a few cows. The roads were flooded, and to top it off, a tree decided to collapse right in front of Ryan's society gate, effectively blocking any chance of me making it out of there. I stared at that fallen tree like it was an omen, both terrified and exhilarated.

I knew what was coming. My dad was going to go into full-on dramatic mode. In his head, if I didn't make it home on time, I was basically starring in *Taken 4*, and Liam Neeson would soon be hunting Ryan down for kidnapping me. I was preparing for the worst, imagining all the wild things my father would say. But Mommy B, my dear soon-to-be mother-in-law, came to the rescue. Like an experienced hostage negotiator, she got on the phone and calmly explained the situation to my parents. With the rain falling in the background and her soothing voice reassuring them, she worked her magic.

It took some time, a few back-and-forths, and probably a lot of deep breathing on my dad's part, but eventually, the verdict was in: I could stay the night. That fallen tree became my knight in shining bark.

Wedding Plans

That night, with the whole house practically giddy from the "breaking of the sleepover curse," Ryan and I stayed up planning our wedding. You know, the usual: discussing possible wedding dates, themes, and colour schemes. Like any engaged couple, we had completely different visions. I was thinking of an elegant, understated ceremony, and Ryan was talking about something that sounded more like the opening scene of *Fast & Furious*. But hey, love is compromise, right?

However, before we could dive headfirst into *our* wedding, my brother's wedding was the next major event on the horizon. My mother and I made a trip to Mumbai to do some shopping for the big day. I was standing in a saree shop when I spotted *the saree*. You know the kind—delicate, netted, and adorned with the most breathtaking crystal work. It was the saree equivalent of love at first sight. I tried on a few others, but nothing could hold a candle to that one. I had found "the one"—saree edition.

The Family Luncheon Disaster

Fast forward to the final week of my brother's wedding preparations, when we hosted Ryan's family at my place for lunch. Everything was going fine until my brother called with some... *news*. His soon-to-be mother-in-law had tested positive for COVID. Just like that, the cheerful lunch became an episode of *Survivor*. My father decided that the only reasonable solution was to ban me from attending the engagement, "for my own safety," of course.

Imagine sitting at a dining table, with Ryan's family on one side, my family on the other, and me smack in the middle, trying to hold back tears. It was like a bad soap opera where everyone's speaking at once, and nobody can hear the protagonist—me, obviously.

My father had made up his mind that I should stay in Pune with Ryan's family while my brother got engaged in Mumbai. But then, in comes my saviour once again – Mommy B. She put her foot down (gently but firmly, of course) and said Ryan and I *would* attend the engagement, and that she and Ryan's dad would join us for the wedding a few days later. Crisis averted, but not without a side of drama.

Mumbai Madness and Grandmother's Blessing

The next day, Ryan and I packed our bags and headed to Mumbai. Ryan, ever the gentleman, stayed at my grandmother's place, and the moment they met, they hit it off. She even said he reminded her of her late husband—talk about winning over the family!

The days leading up to the wedding were a blur of laughter, shopping, and inevitable family drama. I mean, what's a wedding without a little chaos, right? We danced, we laughed, and we dodged last-minute crises. Everything went off without a hitch—or at least, the kind of hitches you just expect with Indian weddings.

The Expressway of Doom (Cue Ominous Music)

After five days of wedding madness, Ryan and I headed back to Pune. As we zoomed down the expressway, I had this weird feeling – a nagging sense that something wasn't right. I brushed it off as post-wedding exhaustion, but I couldn't shake the unease. Later that night, as we were getting ready for bed, I broke down in tears.

Now, I'm not a crier (unless there's a saree sale, of course), but this time, I couldn't stop. Ryan, bless his heart, did his best to calm me down, but the bad feeling wouldn't go away. And guess what? I was right.

COVID Hits: The Unexpected Family Bonding Experience

It all started with a tiny tickle in my throat—nothing alarming at first. But by the next morning, I felt like I had been run over by a truck. Fever, body aches, and a nose that wouldn't stop running. The worst part? We were fresh out of wedding celebrations, having had the time of our lives, and here I was, positive for COVID. I couldn't help but think, "Why now? Just when life was starting to feel perfect."

Ryan, my ever-cautious and paranoid fiancé, immediately freaked out. He insisted on running to the pharmacy to buy every COVID test kit they had, and the results were swift: Positive. Not just me, though. Soon, his father tested positive, and then, as if by some sort of dark irony, Ryan and Mommy B did too. Our little world, which had been filled with the joy and excitement of wedding plans and future dreams, suddenly shrank to the four walls of Ryan's house, now transformed into a quarantine zone.

Emotions Running High: Panic and Fear

The moment the second line appeared on my test, I was hit with an overwhelming mix of emotions—panic, fear, and an absurd sense of guilt. It felt like I had dragged this invisible enemy into Ryan's home, and now we were all paying the price. Ryan's dad, with his slightly serious demeanour, tried to keep calm, but I could see the worry in his eyes.

For Ryan, it was worse. He had this deep-rooted fear of losing his loved ones, a fear that traced back to his childhood. I could see it all over his face—the panic, the dread. It broke my heart because, for the first time, I was the one causing that anxiety. He didn't say it, but I could feel the weight of it in every glance he threw my way, every step he took outside the room where I was quarantined. The look in his eyes said, "Please, let her be okay," but his words were more like, "Stay away; we need to contain this!"

On top of it all, I couldn't stop thinking about my parents. This was the first time I was sick and away from my mom. I hadn't even realised how much I relied on her when I wasn't feeling well. Just the thought of her warm, comforting presence would normally be enough to make me feel better, but here I was, miles away and quarantined. It felt like a cold, cruel joke that I was in my future in-laws' house, sick, without the safety net of my own family.

And then there was the relief. When we all tested positive, it was like a weight was lifted off our shoulders. There was no longer any "What if?" looming over us. We were all in the same boat, and we'd face it together.

The First Few Days: Challenges of Quarantine

The first three days were brutal. I felt miserable, both physically and emotionally. Quarantined in Ryan's room, I was battling fever, body aches, and that insufferable fatigue. My head felt like it was stuffed with cotton, and my body hurt in ways I didn't think were possible. But the worst part wasn't even the physical symptoms—it was the isolation. I couldn't hug Ryan, couldn't be near him, and every time I opened the door to the room, he was standing at the other end of the hall, masked up and staring at me as if he wanted to cry. We both did.

Ryan, with his OCD tendencies, went into full-blown disinfecting mode. He spent the entire day cleaning surfaces, sanitising handles, washing his hands like it was a ritual. I found it both endearing and frustrating. On one hand, I knew it gave him some sense of control in a situation that felt wildly out of our hands, but on the other hand, I just wanted him to be near me. We stood on opposite sides of the door, wishing we could hug, but all we could do was cry and hope that this virus wouldn't take us down.

I've never felt so helpless in my life. I mean, here I was, newly engaged, in the middle of wedding planning, and instead of celebrating, I was worrying about whether we'd all make it out of this in one piece.

The Turning Point: Triumph In the Chaos

Then, something changed. By day four, the fever started to subside, and the panic slowly gave way to acceptance. We were all in this together, and oddly, that gave us a sense of relief. Ryan's mom, ever the peacemaker, started turning our quarantine into a weird version of family bonding. There was nothing we could do about being stuck together, so we decided to make the best of it.

We divided the chores among ourselves. Ryan, naturally, took charge of disinfecting every inch of the house, while Mommy B and I took over the kitchen. We cooked, cleaned, and swapped funny stories between bites of the delicious comfort food we were whipping up. There's something about shared suffering that brings people closer, and this was no exception. In the midst of all the chaos, we found ourselves laughing over the most mundane things—like trying to figure out how to wash dishes without getting too close to each other or who was going to take out the trash in full protective gear.

What made it even more bizarre was the fact that this was happening in the early days of my life with Ryan's family. It's one thing to get to know your future in-laws over casual dinners or family gatherings, but bonding over a global pandemic? Well, that's something else. We got to see each other at our worst—sick, tired, vulnerable, smelly—and somehow, it made us stronger. Ryan's dad, who always seemed a bit formidable, softened up. We had long conversations about everything from life to wedding plans. I was seeing this other side of him, one that was protective and caring in a quiet, understated way.

Ryan and I, too, found a new level of connection. For someone with a fear of losing his loved ones, this was Ryan's worst nightmare, but he was handling it with such grace. Despite all the anxiety and fear, he stood by me, even if it was from a distance. It's one thing to be there for someone in good times, but this was different. I saw in Ryan the kind of strength and resilience I'd always admired, but never experienced quite so intensely.

A Silver Lining in The Pandemic

As weird as it sounds, COVID brought us closer—not just Ryan and me, but our entire family. We became a team, looking out for one another, sharing responsibilities, and offering emotional support. Those ten days of quarantine were a rollercoaster of emotions—fear, exhaustion, frustration—but they were also filled with unexpected moments of joy.

Ryan and I spent countless hours just talking, really talking, about our future, our fears, our hopes. It felt like life had slowed down just enough for us to focus on what really mattered: each other. We laughed at the absurdity of our situation—newly engaged, planning our wedding, and now cooped up together with a virus no one seemed to fully understand.

I remember the moment Ryan and I finally hugged after those long days of separation. It was like the world snapped back into focus—everything was going to be okay.

The Emotional Rollercoaster of Missing Mom

For all the bonding, though, the one thing I couldn't shake was how much I missed my mom. Being sick without her around was a first, and it hit me hard. Sure, Mommy B was an absolute rock, but there's nothing quite like your own mom's hugs when you're feeling crummy.

Ten days later, I finally went home, where my mom was waiting with open arms. That hug was everything. And in that moment, I realised just how much I had grown—learning to cope with chaos, manage life in a joint family, and navigate the never-ending dance between order and, well, total chaos.

The Wedding Countdown Begins: The Frenzy of Preparation

Three months to go, and life was a blur of decisions, colour swatches, and checklists. Weddings are supposed to be fun, right? Well, try planning one while recovering from COVID and fighting a ticking clock. The reality of planning a wedding is far less glamorous than the movies suggest. There's no slow-motion montage with a smiley bride-to-be trying on dresses with perfectly styled hair. Instead, there are sleepless nights, the endless pinging of notifications, and the constant hum of decisions that need to be made. Quickly.

The Venue and Vendors Marathon

First, the venue. Sounds easy, right? But every option we looked at seemed to come with its own set of issues. One was too far for guests, another had an unfortunate colour scheme that couldn't be ignored, and one even had a pigeon problem—trust me, no one wants to get married with birds flying overhead. We finally settled on the fire-temple ground with the banquet hall that felt just right. It had the perfect balance of elegance and charm, though Ryan was mostly sold because the catering was incredible.

Speaking of food—don't even get me started on selecting the menu. Ryan and I had this recurring argument about the starters. I wanted something experimental and fancy, while he insisted on comfort food that would satisfy everyone. "Not everyone wants to eat tiny Chicken farchas, Ryan!" After a few testy back-and-forths, we reached a compromise that, honestly, neither of us fully agreed on, but that's love, right?

The cake tasting, on the other hand, was heavenly. There is something so satisfying about stuffing your face with different flavours of cake while pretending to be on an important mission. Our choice was a two-tiered beauty—chocolate hazelnut, almond caramel with fondant lace, and flowers to match the stage. Cake was something we could easily agree on. In fact, we may have taken the tasting sessions a little too seriously.

Makeup, Florists and Dances: The Details Add Up

The makeup trials were another adventure. Every makeup artist I tried gave me a different look. One made me look like I was auditioning for a vampire movie, while another piled so much highlighter on my face that I could have guided planes. Finally, I found the perfect artist who made me feel like a bride but still like myself. She promised me a flawless, glowing look that would last through tears, heat, and hours of dancing— important for a day filled with emotions.

Dance lessons? Oh, those were fun. Ryan and I had chosen "Almost Paradise" from *Footloose* for our first dance. We thought we were prepared for it—after all, how hard could it be? Well, apparently, much harder than we anticipated. Trying to move in sync, not step on each other's toes, and somehow still look romantic? Let's just say there were plenty of awkward moments, laughter, and more than a few bruised toes. Ryan's lack of rhythm was almost endearing. Almost.

The Emotional Rollercoaster: The Reality of Moving Out

As the wedding day approached, the reality of leaving my home started sinking in. My excitement for the freedom of marriage was dampened by the sadness of packing up my life. I started going through my things—clothes, art supplies, photo albums—and each item seemed to hold a memory. My room, which had always been my sanctuary, was no longer going to be mine.

My future with Ryan was full of possibilities, but leaving behind my family and the life I had known was harder than I had anticipated. I found myself staring at my pillow, the one that had seen countless sleepless nights and emotional meltdowns, and tears started streaming down my face. "Ah, if only the guy had to shift and not us girls," I thought wistfully. The whole process was bittersweet, filled with a mix of excitement and a pang of nostalgia for the life I was leaving behind.

The Naughty Bachelorette and Reality Check

My friends, sensing my emotional rollercoaster, threw me the most epic bachelorette party on our terrace. It was a night of sleazy dancing, embarrassing games, and an unforgettable amount of laughter. We danced until midnight, and the mess we created was monumental. It all started on our terrace, under a canopy of fairy lights. My best friends, all conspirators in this delightful chaos, had transformed the space into a party zone – complete with a dance floor, themed decorations, and let's not forget, the customary phallic-shaped balloons and cake that somehow always make their way to these events (seriously, who started this tradition?). There was a playlist of all the "sexy" songs from the 2000s, a lot of questionable dance moves. The girls had even prepared some games for me – innocent at first, but escalating quickly into more risqué territory.

One of the games involved me being blindfolded and having to guess who was kissing me—well, but, amidst all the laughter, I realised something important. For the first time in a long time, I was able to let loose completely. There was no talk of wedding stress, no discussions about colour themes or flower arrangements. Just pure, unfiltered joy with the people who knew me best. The more the night wore on, the more I could see my single life flashing before my eyes. There was a moment, as I was mid-song, belting out some horribly off-key version of 'Single Ladies' by Beyoncé, that it hit me – I was about to be married! The girl who once found herself navigating messy relationships and unsure of who she was or what she wanted, was now just three days away from saying "I do" to Ryan. It was like I had one foot in my past life, and the other ready to take that step into my future.

But here's the thing about bachelorette parties – they're not all glitter, games, and too much tequila. There's a reality check that sneaks in just when you least expect it. After all the fun had settled and the last of my friends had stumbled out, there I was; Ryan and I left to clean up the aftermath of this wild night.

We laughed, of course, at the absurdity of the night and the chaos left behind; confetti, empty bottles, and God knows how many remnants of the "naughty" decorations that scattered the floor. It was a surreal moment, like the calm after a storm, only this time the storm had been filled with laughter and the calm was filled with something heavier. I looked at Ryan, and it hit me harder than it had before: This was real. We were getting married in just a month. The partying and fun were great, but the gravity of what we were about to do was undeniable.

The next day, Ryan and I dragged ourselves upstairs to clean up, and I couldn't help but laugh at the sheer ridiculousness of the situation.

But life has a way of pulling you back down to earth. That same morning, Ryan and I went to distribute wedding cards. We were at a friend's place when we got a call from Ryan's dad saying Mommy B had almost fainted. Her blood pressure had spiked, and we rushed her to the hospital. The fear in Ryan's eyes was palpable. His OCD-driven anxiety was in full force, and I could see him spiralling. First COVID, now this:

his worst fears seemed to be materialising. I did my best to reassure him that everything would be okay, even though I was shaken too. I had several thoughts flood my mind: fear, panic, anxiety. I had seen Mommy B as a strong rock of a person; was all that going to change? What would be expected of me as a daughter from her? How was I to help someone who was constantly helping me? After a long day of tests, the doctors told us that she had a severe neck issue, but thankfully, nothing life-threatening.

Watching Ryan's silent breakdown made me realise just how much he was carrying – his fears about losing his mom, his worries about the future, and his anxieties about sharing his space and life with me. It was a reminder that while I was dealing with my own anxieties about marriage, he was navigating a massive adjustment too.

In that moment, the reality of marriage hit me like a ton of bricks. It wasn't about the wedding dresses, the songs, the dances, or the cake. It was about this, about being there for each other when life gets messy, when the unexpected happens, when it's not fun or easy. It was about picking up the pieces of each other when one of us felt broken. The wedding was a day, but the marriage. That was a lifetime of facing these moments together. In the end, it was a sobering moment in the whirlwind of wedding preparations, and it brought us closer than ever.

Once Mommy B was on the road to recovery, the focus shifted back to wedding preparations, but something had changed. I was no longer just stressed about planning the perfect day. I was preparing for something bigger than just a celebration. I was preparing for a life where I would have to hold someone up and let them hold me when things went wrong.

So yes, the bachelorette was a night of wild fun and laughter. But the morning after? That was when the real work of building a marriage began. It was a reminder that life doesn't wait for the perfect moment to throw challenges your way. And the biggest lesson I learned? The dance between chaos and order never ends. It's ongoing, unpredictable, and sometimes downright terrifying—but it's also beautiful, especially when you're dancing through it with the right partner.

And at the end of it all, despite everything, I knew I was with the right one.

The Big Day Arrives: A Tornado of Emotions

The morning of the engagement felt surreal. I woke up early, said a prayer, and tried to calm my racing thoughts. "This is it," I thought, "the day my life changes forever." My mom arrived with the traditional silver bowl filled with milk, turmeric, and kumkum, along with flower petals for my ceremonial bath. It was a simple, intimate moment between the two of us, and I could see in her eyes the emotions she was holding back.

The makeup process took three long hours, but the final result was worth it. I looked in the mirror and barely recognised myself. The pink saree with crystal work shimmered under the lights, and the dull gold smoky eyes made me feel like a goddess. Despite my nerves, there was a thrill in the air. I was about to marry Ryan.

The Engagement, Haldi, and Emotional Breakdown

The engagement ceremony was a lively affair, full of music and laughter. Ryan and I exchanged rings with so much excitement; it felt like we were floating. The Haldi ceremony that followed was equally fun, with family members slathering turmeric paste on us, teasing us about married life, and offering well-meaning advice. But by the evening, exhaustion had set in. I was emotionally and physically drained, and all I wanted to do was sleep and not overthink the next day.

Walking Down the Aisle: Tears, Joy, and Love

The day I woke up as a "Contractor" and would sleep as a "Randeria" finally arrived. As the makeup artist worked on me, I couldn't help but feel the weight of the moment. My brother rushed in to announce that Ryan had already arrived and was waiting on stage. "Good, let him wait!" I said with a wink, trying to hide the fact that my heart was racing.

My father, who had been stoic throughout the preparations, finally broke as he held my hand at the aisle. His face was a mixture of pride, love, and the heartbreaking realisation that he was giving his daughter away. As we walked to "Here Comes the Bride," my brother and mother joined us, and we walked together as a family—my whole family, however different we were, giving me away. A moment that will stay with me forever. By the time I reached the stage, I wasn't fighting back tears anymore.

The Ceremony: Hidden "I Love Yous" and A Rice Fight

There we were, sitting opposite each other with a cloth separating us. It was a strange yet intimate moment – surrounded by family and friends, yet in that brief instant, it felt like it was just the two of us. My heart was pounding, and all I could think about was the life we were about to start together. Beneath the cloth, Ryan reached for my hand, and I squeezed it three times. It was our little secret signal for "I love you." He squeezed back, and even though I couldn't see his face, I knew he was smiling.

As the priests chanted prayers, my mind wandered back to all the memories Ryan and I had shared over the years. The ups and downs, the fights, the make-ups, the laughter, and the quiet moments of simply being together. Now, here we were, finally tying the knot, and I couldn't believe it was happening.

The rice-throwing part of the ceremony, where we symbolically shower each other with blessings, was meant to be a simple exchange of rice. But of course, nothing about us is ever that simple. Ryan, ever the mischievous one, launched his rice at me with gusto. I heard a collective gasp from the crowd, followed by laughter. Not to be outdone, I retaliated, but in my defence, my sweaty palms didn't hold enough rice, so my throw was more of a sprinkle than a proper toss. He chuckled, and I knew right then that this playful competitiveness would be a hallmark of our marriage.

At that moment, though surrounded by people, it felt like we were in our own little bubble. The ceremony was unfolding around us, but all I could focus on was the fact that I was finally marrying Ryan, my partner, my best friend. The excitement and emotions were overwhelming.

Congratulations And Celebrations, I Want the World to Know That You're in Love with Me

When the time came to exchange our rings, the air felt thick with emotion. I could hear the murmurs of family members, the shuffling of feet, and the slight crackle of the microphone as we stood facing each other. For a moment, I forgot about everyone else, forgot about the grandeur of the event and the pressure of being in the spotlight.

When we finally exchanged rings, I had to actively stop myself from crying—a rare feat for me. As soon as the rings were on our fingers, we sealed it all with a kiss, and the crowd erupted into applause. It was the most surreal moment of my life. I promised to be his partner in all things, to support him, challenge him, and to never let the laughter leave our lives.

We were officially husband and wife.

The First Dance: Butterflies and Forgetting the Steps

As soon as we were done greeting close family members and exchanging pleasantries, it was time for our first dance. This was one of the moments I had been both looking forward to and dreading. Despite our dance lessons, I was terrified I'd mess up the steps, trip over my saree, or step on Ryan's feet. In the chaos of the day, I could barely remember our choreographed moves.

Ryan, sensing my nervousness, took my hand and whispered, "Just follow my lead." We had chosen the ever-classic *Almost Paradise* from *Footloose* – romantic, timeless, and perfect for the occasion. As soon as the music started, something magical happened. My fears melted away, and for a few minutes, it was like the entire world disappeared. All I could see was Ryan, his eyes locked onto mine, guiding me through each step with a confidence I envied.

It felt like time had slowed down. Everyone around us disappeared into a blur, and it was just us, moving together as one. We may not have nailed every step perfectly, but in that moment, it didn't matter. We were lost in each other's gaze, laughing softly as we twirled and swayed. The butterflies in my stomach were going wild, and for the first time that day, I felt completely at peace.

The crowd cheered as the dance ended, and we shared a quiet, knowing smile. We had survived the dance, and more importantly, we had begun our journey as husband and wife.

The Cake Cutting: Sweet Moments and Perfect Details

Next up was the cake cutting, and if there was one thing I was truly excited about (other than marrying Ryan, of course), it was this. We had chosen a two-tiered masterpiece: chocolate hazelnut with almond caramel, adorned with fondant lace and flowers that matched the stage decor. The cake reflected our personalities – classic, elegant, and just a little bit indulgent.

As we stood in front of the cake, I couldn't help but marvel at the details. The lace fondant matched my saree so perfectly that I almost didn't want to cut into it. Almost. But the temptation of chocolate and caramel won out, and together, Ryan and I made the first cut, smiling at each other as we did. The room filled with cheers, and we fed each other a small piece, the sweetness of the cake matching the sweetness of the moment.

The next few hours were a whirlwind of meet-and-greets, hugs, and laughter. We barely had time to eat, but that didn't matter – this was the happiest I'd been in a long time, and the adrenaline was carrying me through.

The Photoshoot: Fun, Friends, and Posing Like Pros

Before the night ended, it was time for the couples' photoshoot, and as someone who lives for photos, I was beyond excited. Despite being utterly exhausted, I summoned every last bit of energy I had left for the shoot. Ryan, ever the trooper, joined me in striking a variety of poses – from the classic romantic shots to the more playful ones that had us both cracking up.

We posed with friends, family, and even managed to sneak in a few fun candid shots that perfectly captured the joy of the evening. By the end of it, we were starving, but every photo was worth it. The photographers were amazing, capturing moments I didn't even realise had happened.

Saying Goodbye: The Bittersweet Farewell

After the photos and the endless rounds of congratulations, it was time for the hardest part of the night – saying goodbye to my family. The reality of leaving my home, my parents, and my brother behind hit me like a ton of bricks. I hugged my mom tightly, tears streaming down both our faces. My dad, always the stoic one, tried his best to keep it together, but I could see the emotion in his eyes. He hugged me longer than usual, his grip firm as if he wasn't ready to let go.

My brother, who had been my rock throughout the entire process, gave me a hug that said everything – he was proud of me, and even though we'd always bickered growing up, I knew he was going to miss me just as much as I'd miss him. It was one of those rare moments of sibling tenderness that you never forget.

Meher had always been my biggest cheerleader, standing by me through every chapter of my life. As the moment arrived for Ryan and me to leave for the evening as a newly married couple, I found myself searching for her in the crowd. When our eyes met, we didn't need words to communicate what we were feeling. In an instant, I rushed towards her and hugged her tightly, holding on as if letting go would mean leaving behind a part of me.

We both burst into tears, tears of joy, nostalgia, and the bittersweet realisation that everything was changing. It was the kind of change we had talked about since we were kids, imagining what our future weddings would look like, the kind of people we would marry, and how we'd stand beside each other no matter what. And now, it was all happening. It wasn't just a dream anymore. The wedding had happened, and I was stepping into a new chapter of my life.

The funny part—the part that made me smile through my tears—was how seamlessly Meher had transitioned from "My Team" to Team Ryan. It was almost as if she had been waiting for this moment as much as I had, eagerly joining forces with him to make my life even better. In her own bubbly, giddy-headed way, Meher was now on his side too, teasing me about how I was "outnumbered" by my two favourite people in the world.

As we wiped away our tears, I realised that even though so much had changed, the essence of our bond remained untouched. The joy, the humour, and the unwavering support Meher gave me weren't going anywhere – they were just expanding to include Ryan in the mix. And honestly, my life was that much richer because of it.

As I climbed into the car with Ryan, a wave of mixed emotions washed over me. I was leaving behind a part of myself, a chapter of my life that had shaped me into who I was. But at the same time, I was stepping into a new adventure, with the man I loved by my side. Ryan gently kissed me on the lips and whispered, "Hello, Wifey." Butterflies erupted in my stomach, and I couldn't help but smile.

The After-Party: Cake, Champagne and Family Traditions

The night wasn't over yet. When we arrived at Ryan's house, the family had gathered for a small after-party, complete with cake and champagne. It was a warm, intimate gathering, a stark contrast to the grand ceremony we had just come from. We laughed, shared stories, and celebrated the fact that we had made it through the day.

As part of tradition, each family member came to our room to bless us before we wound up for the night. It was a sweet gesture, but by the time the last person had left, I was ready to collapse. I had never been so exhausted, yet so happy in my life.

The Final Moments: A Quiet End to A Perfect Day

Finally, after what felt like the longest day of my life, Ryan and I retreated to our bedroom. To my surprise, Mommy B had decorated the room with rose petals and lit my favourite vanilla-scented candle. It was the perfect, cosy ending to an otherwise chaotic day.

Ryan, ever the gentleman, helped me take out the million bobby pins from my hair, and I peeled off my makeup and jewellery, relishing the feeling of freedom. After a long, warm bath, I slipped into bed beside him, the weight of the day finally lifting off my shoulders.

We lay there in silence, simply enjoying each other's presence. There was no need for words – we were finally together, married, and ready to start the rest of our lives. Before I knew it, I drifted off to sleep, my heart full, knowing I was exactly where I was meant to be.

Lessons Learned: Letting Go and Embracing the Dance Between Chaos and Order

Reflecting on this chapter of my life, the journey to marriage taught me that love, commitment, and life itself are never straightforward. They're a dance, a constant give and take between the chaos of the unexpected and the order we try to impose on our world. And the truth is, no matter how much we plan, life will always find a way to surprise us. The wedding preparations were proof enough—there were moments where I thought everything was under control, only to have it turned upside down by a sudden crisis, like a fainting spell, last-minute COVID scares, or emotional meltdowns. But through all the madness, there were moments of clarity and joy.

I realised that the key to surviving these moments wasn't about controlling every little detail, but about learning to flow with the chaos. And Ryan and I did that: we learned to laugh when things went off track, to lean on each other when the weight of the world felt too heavy, and to find peace amidst the disorder. We didn't get through it by having everything perfectly aligned; we got through it by holding each other's hands and saying, "We'll figure this out together."

The biggest lesson I took from this period is that life's chaos isn't something to be feared; it's something to be embraced. In fact, the chaos is what makes life real. It brings out our vulnerabilities, our raw emotions, and forces us to adapt. The order—the structure we create through plans and expectations—gives us stability. But it's the chaotic moments that make us grow, that test our strength and resolve. Without the unexpected twists and turns, there would be no learning, no deepening of love.

Ryan and I didn't just vow to love each other in the best of times; we vowed to support each other when everything seemed to be falling apart. We vowed to find balance when life felt like a whirlwind. And that balance came from trusting each other and trusting the process. Through the rice fights, the hidden "I love you" beneath the wedding cloth, and the long nights of wedding planning, I learned that marriage isn't about the perfect ceremony or the picture-perfect relationship. It's about how you handle the imperfections and unexpected challenges.

The dance between chaos and order became our rhythm, sometimes chaotic, sometimes orderly, but always in sync. There's a beauty in that, in knowing that life will never be predictable, but that you've found someone who will weather the storms with you, who will laugh with you when things go awry, and who will hold you steady when the ground feels shaky.

Ultimately, the wow-factor isn't just the promises we made to each other at the altar; it's the everyday vows we continue to make. The vow to embrace the chaos, to let go of the need for control, and to trust that together, we can navigate anything that comes our way. It's the vow to dance through life's highs and lows, knowing that as long as we're dancing together, we'll find our way back to order, no matter how many times we stumble along the way.

So, the greatest learning from this chapter is that life is messy, unpredictable, and beautifully chaotic. And love—real love—is about accepting that mess and choosing, every single day, to keep dancing through it. Whether it's planning a wedding, dealing with family drama, or navigating personal struggles, it's about knowing that there's no perfect order to things. There's just the dance, and the joy that comes from sharing that dance with someone who is willing to embrace the chaos with you.

A Note from Present Me to 20-Year-Old Me

Dear 20-Something-Year-Old Me,

I know you're feeling overwhelmed right now. Life seems like an endless maze, doesn't it? You've got big dreams, bigger fears, and you're trying to hold onto control in a world that seems determined to knock you off balance. You're probably wondering when it all falls into place, when things become simple, when the chaos subsides. Here's the spoiler: it doesn't.

But before you panic, hear me out — there's a kind of magic in the chaos. It won't always feel this overwhelming. In fact, the things that seem like a storm right now will one day be the very moments you smile back on. You'll learn that life isn't about waiting for the storm to pass or trying to make everything fit perfectly. Life is about dancing in the storm, embracing the uncertainty, and finding strength in the mess.

Right now, you think love will be this smooth, perfect ride — that once you meet "the one," everything will just fall into place. I hate to break it to you, but love, just like life, is chaotic too. There will be moments of frustration when you're fighting because neither of you knows how to handle the pressure of the world bearing down. There will be times when everything feels uncertain and messy, and you'll feel like you're failing at all of it. But those moments? They're also the moments that will make your love stronger, more real, more grounded.

You'll learn that love isn't about perfection; it's about showing up. It's about holding someone's hand in the middle of the chaos, even when it feels like you can barely hold yourself together. It's about giving yourself grace when you mess up—and trust me, you'll mess up plenty—and giving the same grace to the person you love. The beauty in love comes not from the moments when everything is smooth sailing, but in the times when you've both weathered a storm and found each other on the other side, stronger, more connected, more in sync.

There's something else I want you to know: the things you fear most—losing control, things not going according to plan—those are the very things that will teach you who you really are. They will shape you into someone who is resilient, who can handle the unknown without crumbling. The moments when everything falls apart will give you the chance to rebuild, and in that rebuilding, you'll find parts of yourself you didn't even know existed. You'll realise that chaos isn't something to be afraid of; it's something to embrace. It's life's way of showing you just how strong you are.

And you'll find out that love, in all its messy, imperfect glory, is worth every ounce of chaos. It's worth the uncertainty, the moments of doubt, and the unexpected twists and turns. Because in the end, love isn't about controlling the dance – it's about finding joy in it, even when the rhythm feels off.

Looking back, I wish I could tell you that everything will fall neatly into place. But the truth is, life will always be a balance between chaos and order. And that's okay. You'll learn to find peace in that balance. You'll realise that the dance between chaos and order isn't something to fight against; it's something to lean into. Because that's where life happens – in the space between the plans and the surprises, the control and the unknown.

So, dear 20-Something-Year-Old Me, stop trying to have it all figured out. You won't, and that's okay. Embrace the mess. Learn to dance in it. Trust that you'll find your way, not because everything will be perfect, but because you'll learn to thrive in the imperfection. And one day, you'll look back and realise that the chaos wasn't your enemy — it was your teacher.

Keep dancing, my love. You've got this.

With all my heart,

Your Future Self

Chapter 7

The Struggle Is Real – Mental, Physical Health, And Self-Care When You're Forced to Make Life-Altering Changes

In echoes of conflict, she faced her past,
With grit and with grace, she stood steadfast.
Through shattered dreams and broken ties,
She learned that true healing can only arise.
In the chaos of change, her spirit found peace,
From battles within, she sought her release.
Forgiveness and growth were her guiding stars,
She emerged renewed, with wisdom from scars.

The Honeymoon Phase Ends (and Reality Kicks In)

Ah, the honeymoon phase. That magical time when your new spouse can do no wrong, and every little quirk they have is *adorable*. The way Ryan insisted on folding his socks with military precision? Adorable. The way he put ketchup on literally everything, including pasta? Endearing. Fast forward to week three of marital bliss, and let me tell you, the magic starts to wear off quicker than you can say, *"Where's my space?"*

We came back from our honeymoon, tanned, relaxed, and ready to take on life as a dream team. I had visions of us as that perfect, Instagram-worthy couple who'd tackle the world with love and matching outfits. What I didn't anticipate was that "taking on life" meant adjusting to living with *five* other people. That's right—suddenly, I wasn't just responsible for navigating the joys of being a newlywed but also for navigating the lives of my in-laws and grandparents-in-law.

Now, don't get me wrong. Ryan's family is lovely. Kind, generous, and always supportive. But when you're used to the freedom of living alone, sharing a house with your husband, his parents, *and* his grandparents is like being cast in a sitcom where you're both the protagonist and the punchline.

Every day felt like an unspoken game of "What Time Will She Snap Today?" No one *made* me do anything around the house—there were no mandatory chores or cooking schedules—but I felt the *unofficial* responsibility creeping in. And so, in a desperate attempt to make a good impression and not be labelled "the lazy daughter-in-law," I made it my personal mission to wake up earlier than the entire household and become the self-proclaimed *Tea Fairy*.

While they never forced me into any household duties, I thought it was a good time to ease into them gradually. I started small—waking up just a tad earlier than the rest of the family to make tea. Now, tea-making was sacred. It wasn't just a morning routine; it was a ritual. And I wanted to make sure I nailed it. If there's one thing you don't mess up in an Indian household, it's the morning chai. I also packed Ryan's lunch bag and prepared his breakfast, leaving a tiny love note in his bag, with something cheesy like, *"Good luck at work today, my love. Remember, I'm cuter than your colleagues!"* A tiny gesture, but hey, every relationship needs a bit of *Hallmark card* humour, right? You know, the newlywed stuff you do before the realities of marriage settle in, and you start questioning why you ever agreed to cook and pack lunch.

Everything was great—until, well, it wasn't. The euphoria of marriage, the little joys of making tea and sneaking love notes began to fade as we both got engrossed in our daily work routines. And before we knew it, the weekend date nights turned into, "Let's just sleep in, I'm too tired," or "Maybe next week, babe." But that's life, isn't it? You get caught up in the whirlwind of adulting. Work, chores, and family commitments became the routine, and we knew we had to do something to keep the spark alive. So, we made a pact—every weekend, no matter how busy, we would go on a date. It was non-negotiable, a little bubble of *us* time amidst the whirlwind of family life. Whether it was a cosy movie night at home or a fancy dinner out, we made sure to keep that one night sacred for just the two of us.

Living In a Joint Family Is Like Reality TV Without the Cameras

Living in a joint family was no joke. It was like starring in my own personal reality show, except there were no cameras (but oh, the judging eyes). And don't get me wrong; I had the freedom to live life the way I wanted. But there's something about having four other family members around that makes you hyper-aware of every little thing you do. It was like being in a fishbowl—everyone could see everything, and I was constantly overthinking how I spoke to Ryan, what I wore, how I behaved.

Ryan and I were, of course, madly in love, but we were also human, which meant we had our share of disagreements. And let me tell you, being newly married and living in a joint family can make even the tiniest argument feel like World War III. We had our differences, and while I had grown up in a household where raising your voice was second nature, Ryan was the exact opposite. Raised in a calm, composed household, he hated yelling. The moment my voice rose above normal volume, I could see his brain switch off. I had to quickly learn to stay calm, to communicate without the drama. Trust me, it wasn't easy, especially when you've grown up fighting for your voice to be heard.

Marriage Adjustment: Welcome To the OCD Zone

Dating someone and living with them 24/7 are two entirely different realities. I had known Ryan for a while, but it wasn't until we shared a home that I began to understand his quirks, habits, and—dare I say—obsessions. You know, like his near-OCD tendencies to keep everything organised. My casual "I'll get to it later" approach didn't sit well with him, and I quickly realised that in Ryan's world, "later" meant "never." He was the king of structure and organisation, and I, well, was more of a "let's wing it" kind of person.

At first, I resisted his insistence on doing things a certain way. I had spent years learning to live around restrictions in my own home, and the thought of having to adjust to a new set of "rules" didn't sit well with me. I felt like I was right, and he was being overly rigid. But here's the thing—I wasn't in my past anymore. I had married Ryan because I loved him, and I knew we needed to find a balance.

Old Habits Die Hard (Especially Yelling)

Ryan's obsessive need to control things around him stemmed from a deep-seated fear of losing the people he loved. I could see it, but at the time, it felt suffocating. Every disagreement we had felt magnified because we couldn't argue without it spilling over into the rest of the family. Living in a house with four other people meant that our fights became everyone's business. I couldn't help but draw parallels between Ryan and my father. The fear of losing control, the anxiety about health—both had their roots in a place of love, but they manifested in ways that made me feel like I was walking on eggshells. Ryan wasn't my father. I didn't have to fight tooth and nail for everything. Yet, I still found myself slipping into old patterns of behaviour, raising my voice, and making matters worse. I remember one day when Ryan and I had an especially bad argument, and Mommy B stepped in as the peacemaker. She tried to be fair, but no matter whose side she took, it was clear that it wasn't fair to constantly put her in the middle of our marital squabbles.

And here's where things got tricky. My natural instinct was to yell when I felt like I wasn't being heard. But Ryan? He couldn't stand it. One day, after a particularly heated argument,

Ryan—calm, composed Ryan—looked me in the eye and with a very stern voice, said he wouldn't tolerate being disrespected. That was a wake-up call. I hadn't realised how much my tone, my words, and my body language were affecting him. It wasn't just the argument itself; it was the way I was arguing that was causing damage.

Learning To Fight Fair (Or At Least Quieter)

After that day, we made a pact. We wouldn't let fights drag on forever. We instituted a 30-minute timer from the moment we started arguing. Once the 30 minutes were up, we had to make amends—no matter how much we wanted to sulk. And guess what? It actually worked. Most of the time, Ryan was the one to apologise first, but it wasn't long before I learned that apologising didn't mean admitting defeat. It meant prioritising peace.

Ryan and I also started a little system—every day we didn't fight, we'd put a smiley face on the calendar. And on the days when one of us had upset the other, we'd mark a sad face. It sounds silly, but tracking our moods helped us become more mindful of how we were treating each other. Soon, the days of sad faces became fewer and fewer, and we didn't need the chart anymore.

The Decision to Start a Family

Very soon after our wedding, Ryan and I decided it was time to start trying to conceive. We did a lot of thinking, planning, and dreaming about what life would look like with a baby.

It was an exciting step for us both, though Ryan seemed more prepared than I was. Still, we felt that we were ready to welcome a little bundle of joy into our lives. Little did we know, life was about to throw us a curveball that would put all our plans on hold.

The Health Scare That Changed Everything

As the months passed, we settled into a routine. Ryan and I continued our date nights, and everything seemed to be going smoothly until it wasn't. I had been working long hours at my desk job, and the lack of exercise started catching up to me. I'd wake up with a stiff neck more often than not, and soon enough, it became impossible to ignore. The situation quickly escalated, and I found myself visiting a chiropractor for temporary relief. However, as the months passed, the discomfort would always return, and I had to keep going back.

Ryan had already been dealing with his mother's neck issues, and now here I was, following in her footsteps. His anxiety skyrocketed, and honestly, so did mine. He didn't just have one person in the family with neck problems; now he had two. And let me tell you, when Ryan gets anxious, it's like living with a tornado that's about to touch down. He couldn't handle the idea of something happening to me, and I knew I had to do something about it. So, I started slow—really slow. I tried incorporating exercise into my routine, but it wasn't helping much.

Then, one morning, I woke up, and I couldn't move. My neck was so stiff that even breathing hurt. Ryan had to literally carry me out of bed and help me to the bathroom.

It was humiliating. Here I was, not even a year into our marriage, and Ryan had to deal with me like I was some kind of invalid. The pain wasn't just in my neck anymore; it had started shooting down my arms. One orthopaedic doctor after another delivered the same bad news: I had wrecked my spine through years of bad posture, poor work habits, and a complete lack of exercise.

I was diagnosed with severe cervical spasm and degeneration. Every test I took confirmed the same thing. The prognosis was bleak. The doctor told me in no uncertain terms that as long as I continued my desk job, my condition would only get worse. I was ordered complete bed rest and intensive spine therapy for 15 days.

The Pain of Letting Go

This was a major turning point in my life. Ryan, who had been my rock through it all, insisted that I quit my job and focus on recovery. He reminded me that without my health, we couldn't even think about having a baby. He was right, of course, but the thought of quitting my job devastated me. I had always been an ambitious woman. I thrived on my financial independence and took great pride in my work. Now, it seemed like all of that was slipping away. My dreams of a promotion were vanishing, and with them, our plans to start a family were put on indefinite hold.

The first 15 days of bed rest were brutal. Not just physically, but emotionally and mentally. I felt trapped in a body that wasn't cooperating with me. Every small movement felt like a battle. And worst of all, I felt like I was a burden to

Ryan. This man, who had married me with hopes and dreams for our future, was now stuck dealing with a wife who could barely get out of bed. The guilt gnawed at me constantly.

Ryan, bless his heart, did everything he could to keep my spirits up. After work, he would come home and take me for a walk, even though I was terrified of walking alone, afraid something would happen. That time in my life was one of the darkest periods I've ever experienced. I was in physical pain, my mental health was suffering, and I was overwhelmed by a sense of hopelessness. The job I loved and the dreams we had for our future seemed so far out of reach.

Making Exercise My Best Friend

It was during this time that I started to turn to exercise, not just as a form of rehabilitation, but as a lifeline. I realised that if I was going to get better, I had to strengthen my body. There was no other option. I made exercise my best friend, even though every step felt like a struggle. Slowly but surely, I committed to strengthening my muscles, focusing on small steps toward recovery. But while my physical strength was gradually improving, my emotional and spiritual health needed just as much attention.

Turning to Faith for Strength

In the quiet moments of bed rest, I began praying to Jesus, asking Him what lessons I was supposed to learn from this season of suffering. I had never felt more vulnerable or lost, and I needed guidance. One evening, Ryan noticed I seemed deep in thought and asked me what was on my mind. That's when I decided to open up to him about something I had kept to myself for a long time—my faith.

I shared with Ryan how important my relationship with Jesus was to me, how He had helped me through so many difficult times in the past, and how I believed that Ryan was in my life because I had prayed for him. I also told him about how my parents hadn't taken my faith seriously, and I had been hesitant to share it with him for fear of rejection.

To my surprise, Ryan didn't react negatively at all. In fact, he asked why I hadn't told him sooner. His openness made me feel a weight lift off my shoulders.

Meeting PDJ: A Life-Changing Encounter

After months of intense personal struggle and deep reflection, a pivotal moment arrived that would forever alter the course of my life and marriage. My mentor, PDJ, who had been a guiding light during my spiritual journey, was returning to India after a long hiatus due to the pandemic. This news was met with a mix of excitement and reverence, as PDJ had been a significant influence on my faith and personal growth.

Ryan, having observed my spiritual journey from a distance, noticed how important this meeting was to me. His curiosity about my faith and his desire to support me were growing stronger. When I shared the news of PDJ's return, Ryan insisted that we make the trip to see him. I was thrilled at the prospect of introducing Ryan to someone who had played such a crucial role in my life and faith.

The day of the meeting with PDJ was charged with anticipation. We arrived at the venue, a place that was both familiar and sacred to me, filled with memories of spiritual growth and community. PDJ's presence was as comforting as ever, radiating a sense of calm and wisdom that I had always admired.

I introduced Ryan to PDJ, and there was an immediate sense of connection. Ryan's initial apprehension gave way to genuine curiosity and respect as he engaged in conversation with PDJ. It was a moment of immense significance, as I saw Ryan opening up to the world of faith that had been such an integral part of my life.

A Prayer for Healing

As we were about to leave, PDJ asked if he could pray for us. This simple gesture was imbued with profound meaning. He prayed not only for our personal struggles but specifically for my neck and complete healing. It was the first time Ryan had witnessed such a powerful and heartfelt prayer. He could feel the presence of God in a way he hadn't experienced before.

For me, this was a moment of deep emotional release. I had been carrying a heavy burden of anxiety and pain, and PDJ's prayer was like a balm to my weary soul. It was as if the weight of my struggles was being lifted, and I felt a renewed sense of hope and peace.

A New Chapter for Ryan

The drive home from the meeting was filled with a palpable change in Ryan. He was visibly moved, and there was a newfound calmness in him. Later that night, Ryan shared with me how the experience had impacted him deeply. He admitted that he had always wanted to experience the presence of God but had never truly felt it until that day.

This revelation was a turning point for us as a couple. Ryan's openness to exploring faith and his desire to learn more about Jesus were transformative. It was as if the prayer had unlocked a new dimension of understanding for him, bridging the gap between our individual spiritual journeys and our shared faith.

In the weeks that followed, Ryan's newfound interest in faith became a central theme in our lives. We began reading the Bible together, exploring its teachings, and discussing our spiritual insights. This shared exploration brought us closer together, creating a deeper bond rooted in mutual respect and understanding.

The meeting with PDJ had not only impacted Ryan's faith journey but had also reinforced the strength of our relationship. It was a reminder that faith could be a unifying force, capable of bringing clarity and peace amidst life's trials. Our conversations and shared spiritual practices became a source of comfort and connection, helping us navigate the challenges we faced with renewed strength.

A Journey of Faith

As we continued to navigate the challenges of my health and our plans for the future, the impact of our meeting with PDJ remained a guiding light. Ryan's faith journey evolved, and he became more proactive in seeking spiritual growth and support. Our prayers for peace, healing, and guidance became an integral part of our daily lives.

The encounter with PDJ was a pivotal moment that transformed not only Ryan's perspective but also our relationship. It reinforced the idea that faith, prayer, and spiritual guidance could provide solace and direction during even the most difficult times. Meeting PDJ was more than just a reunion; it was a profound encounter that reshaped our spiritual journey and strengthened our bond as a couple. It was a reminder of the power of faith to bring about change, heal wounds, and foster deeper connections. This life-changing moment marked a new chapter in our lives, one characterised by a shared commitment to faith, growth, and mutual support.

A New Career Path with Ryan's Mother

A few months later, as I regained some of my strength, Ryan's mother approached me with an opportunity. She asked if I would like to help her with her business, and I was thrilled. It gave me something to look forward to and allowed me to stay productive while I continued to recover. Not only did she offer me flexible hours, but she also paid me for my work.

I found myself enjoying the work more than I had expected. I began creating content for her business, writing blogs, handling her marketing team, and even exploring new avenues for her brand. Within a month, I felt a renewed sense of purpose. The work gave me something positive to focus on, and I slowly began regaining my physical strength as well.

Ryan's Transformation: Letting Go of Control

During this period, Ryan also went through a significant transformation. He had always been someone who tried to control every aspect of life, but he began to realise that he couldn't always manage the inevitable. Watching me go through this health crisis and relying on God for strength changed his perspective. He started letting go of the need to control everything and instead relied on Jesus for peace and guidance.

We prayed together for healing, for peace, and for freedom from doubt. Most importantly, we surrendered our plans for having a baby to God. We trusted that His timing was perfect and that everything would happen when it was meant to.

A Turning Point in Our Lives

Looking back, this period of our lives was one of the most challenging, yet it was also one of the most transformative. Ryan found peace in his faith, I discovered a new passion in my career, and we grew closer as a couple, united by our faith and love for each other. We had reached a turning point—a moment where we realised that even in the darkest times, there is always hope, healing, and the promise of new beginnings.

This was the chapter in our lives that marked a transition, not just for me physically, but for both of us spiritually. It was a time of surrender, growth, and ultimately, a deeper connection with each other and with God.

A Note from Present Me to 20-Year-Old Me

Dear 20-Something-Year-Old Me,

I'm writing to you from a place you might find hard to imagine right now. I know you're brimming with dreams, energy, and a desire to conquer the world, but I want to share something crucial with you—a glimpse into a future you will experience and the lessons you'll learn along the way.

At 20, you're vibrant and full of ambition, balancing school, work, and the pressures of family life. You think you have everything figured out, but life has a way of throwing unexpected challenges your way. I want to tell you about a pivotal chapter that will unfold in your life—one that will test you in ways you can't yet foresee.

Soon, you'll decide it's time to start a family with the love of your life. It will be an exciting time, filled with hope and dreams. But life has other plans, and you will face a significant health crisis that will turn your world upside down. Your desk job, which once seemed manageable, will become a source of debilitating pain. Your neck will become a constant reminder of the price of your sedentary lifestyle, and you'll be forced to confront a harsh reality.

The pain will become so severe that it will stop you in your tracks. You'll struggle with daily tasks, and the fear of being a burden to your loved ones will weigh heavily on your heart. This period will be incredibly challenging—one that will test your resilience and force you to re-evaluate your priorities. You'll have to make the difficult decision to leave your job, a place where you had once felt proud and ambitious. The transition will be painful, both physically and emotionally, but it will also be a time of profound personal growth.

In the midst of this crisis, you will discover the power of faith. You'll find solace in your spiritual beliefs, and this newfound strength will become a beacon of hope. Your relationship with your husband will deepen as he too begins to explore faith and find peace in it. This journey will bring you closer together and shift your perspective on life.

You will also find a new purpose in unexpected places. Working with Ryan's mother, you'll discover a passion for creating content and contributing in meaningful ways. This opportunity will not only help you recover but also reignite your sense of purpose and creativity.

I want you to know that this period of hardship will be transformative. It will teach you the importance of surrender, faith, and finding strength in unexpected places. You'll learn to let go of control and trust in a greater plan. The challenges you face will ultimately lead you to a deeper understanding of yourself, your relationships, and your faith.

So, embrace the journey with an open heart. The road ahead may be difficult, but it will also be filled with moments of profound growth and unexpected blessings. Trust that you are exactly where you need to be, and know that even in the darkest times, there is always hope and light to be found.

With love and understanding,

Your Future Self

Chapter 8

Bun In the Oven: The Unexpected Surprise

Through sleepless nights and trials so grand,
She welcomed new life with a trembling hand.
In the heart of the storm, she found her light,
Her strength, her courage, shining bright.
From joyful chaos to the tender embrace,
She discovered love in its purest grace.
In every challenge, a lesson she'd weave,
Her heart full of hope, with dreams to achieve.

The Calm Before The... Baby?

Six months post-neck incident, I was on the upswing – gaining strength, happy, and finally at peace. So, naturally, Ryan and I decided to take a much-needed trip abroad. After all, we had survived the neck drama, emotional rollercoasters, and enough stress to fuel a soap opera. This vacation was our ticket to fun and relaxation.

We crafted an itinerary packed with rollercoasters, desert safaris, and maybe some *responsible* relaxation. Everything was set, except for one looming factor: my period was due that week. Fantastic. Just what every woman dreams of when she's about to dune dash through a desert—menstrual cramps.

The Test of Curiosity

It was the night before our trip. I was casually packing, triple-checking that I had all the necessary documents and making sure Ryan didn't forget his socks. (Men and socks on trips are a mystery I'll never solve.) Meanwhile, my period was three days late, which wasn't exactly breaking news in my life, but for some insane reason, I thought, "Why not pee on a stick? Just for fun."

I wasn't remotely concerned. Ten days prior, I'd had a fever and a urine test that flatly told me I wasn't pregnant. So, logically, I wasn't expecting anything. Until... two faint pink lines showed up. **WHAT?**

I squinted at the test like it was an ancient map leading me to treasure. And then it hit me: **Oh my gosh, I'm pregnant!** Cue the heart-thumping, breath-shaking, movie-worthy scene where the protagonist drops to her knees and thanks the heavens. I, the protagonist in this case, thanked God, then immediately spiralled into a panic.

"Wait a second—what about tomorrow? What about the rollercoasters? Should we cancel them all? And... should we tell our parents?" I zoomed over to Mommy

B like I was auditioning for an Olympic relay. We both squealed like teenagers at a boy band concert and rushed to buy three more pregnancy tests because, apparently, one wasn't enough. All three came back positive. Yep, definitely pregnant.

"Hello, Daddy!"

While waiting for Ryan to come home, I decided to get creative. I placed the positive tests on the bathroom counter with a note that said, "Hello, Daddy." When he finally walked through the door, I casually whipped out my phone and started recording his reaction.

The second he saw the note, he burst into tears like a Hallmark commercial. We hugged so tightly, I thought we might fuse together. There we stood, sobbing and grinning, thanking God for this unbelievable surprise.

Reality, though, doesn't stay suspended in pure joy for too long. After wiping away the happy tears, we sat down to make some very necessary changes to our itinerary. Desert Safari? Cancelled. Rollercoasters? Well, I wouldn't ride any. Instead, we prepared for a vacation filled with... walking and snacks. Lots of snacks.

Airport Drama: Snack Attack

The next morning, we were at the airport, all set to embark on our vacation. Everything was smooth sailing until I felt my blood sugar drop faster than my patience during pregnancy. I got dizzy, and Ryan—God bless him—went into full

"Superman mode," running around the airport at 5 a.m., trying to find food. But guess what? **Nothing was open**. Classic.

After some pleading with a staff member, we managed to get our hands on a sad little packet of chips - which I devoured like it was gourmet cuisine. Crisis averted; we made it to our gate. Once we arrived at our destination, the exhaustion of being newly pregnant hit me like a truck. So much for a "relaxing vacation"—I was already feeling like I'd run a marathon.

The Vacation That Turned into A Naptime Marathon

Upon arrival, I realised something: pregnancy exhaustion is no joke. Every activity we did—whether it was sightseeing or having a meal—required a post-event nap. Rollercoasters were out; naps were in. Ryan and I quickly learned that this trip was going to be more about rest than adrenaline, which was fine by me. At least I had a legitimate excuse for bailing on all those scary rides. However, we did thoroughly enjoy our trip. We had our days of rest and our days of adventure.

The Baby Makes Its First Appearance

Once we got home, we went straight to the gynaecologist, who confirmed that we were officially 6 weeks and 2 days pregnant. Our little baby was the size of a rice grain, and the tiny heartbeat flashing on the screen had us in tears all over again. I was in love—deep, overwhelming, all-consuming love for this little peanut. Sorry, Ryan, but this love was on a whole new level.

We headed to my parents' house to drop the bombshell. The moment I handed them the ultrasound, it was like fireworks went off. My dad jumped and shouted like a teenager, while my mom clung to me as if I were her personal emotional support pillow. Then we broke the news to Ryan's grandparents, who were *over the moon*. "We get to play with our great-grandchild!" they exclaimed, looking as excited as kids on Christmas morning.

Next up: informing the rest of the family. It was all hugs, tears, and awkward conversations about how much my life was about to change.

The Best Birthday Surprise: Meher Becomes a Masi

After we returned from our trip, Ryan and I were eager to share some exciting news with Meher. We had picked out a special birthday gift for her, but what she didn't know was that we had something even bigger in store – a surprise that would change her life just as much as it had changed ours.

We decided to meet at our usual hangout spot, and after catching up on life and sharing stories from our trip, it was time for the big reveal. In her gift bag, among the souvenirs and goodies we had picked up for her, I had hidden the tiniest pair of baby socks with a little tag attached that read, "Happy Birthday, Masi!"

When I handed over the bag and asked her to open it, she casually began rummaging through the gifts. But the moment she saw those tiny socks and the tag, her eyes widened in shock, followed quickly by a flood of tears. In true Meher fashion, she let out a joyous scream and flung herself at me, enveloping me in the tightest, most emotional hug I'd ever received.

Then, just as quickly, she turned to Ryan, squeezing him in a bear hug, tears still streaming down her face, as she shouted between sobs, "This is the best birthday gift ever!" It was such a pure, raw moment of joy, one that I will cherish forever.

After calming down slightly, Meher placed her hand gently on my tummy, already showering our baby with love and blessings. She promised right then and there that she would spoil our little one rotten, and knowing Meher, I had no doubt she would. In that moment, Meher wasn't just my best friend anymore—she had officially become "Masi," and the bond between us deepened in a way that only such life-changing moments can bring.

The Real Rollercoaster: Pregnancy Brain and Mood Swings

Then, the rollercoaster of pregnancy symptoms began. First came the fatigue. I was perpetually tired. Then the nausea kicked in—not the glamorous, movie-style morning sickness. Nope, this was a 24/7 nausea-fest. And don't even get me started on the mood swings. I was an emotional landmine. Poor Ryan had no idea whether he'd come home to hugs or a hysterical breakdown over an empty jar of pickles.

To top it off, my hunger became insatiable. I wasn't craving dainty little snacks; I wanted greasy burgers and spicy Chinese food. It was like my body had turned into a bottomless pit, and my appetite was on a world tour. But while I was indulging, I was also freaking out. The anxiety was *real*. I couldn't exercise because of the risk of aggravating my neck injury, and that terrified me. I was consumed with the fear that my neck would betray me, and I wouldn't have the strength to carry this baby.

What if I lost the baby because I was weak? What if not having typical pregnancy symptoms, like vomiting, meant something was wrong? The what-ifs were endless, and the thought of not being able to work out added fuel to the fire.

As if my body wasn't being enough of a drama queen, my brain decided to join the party. Pregnancy brain is a *real* thing, and I was its prime victim. I couldn't remember where I put anything. Once, I yelled at Ryan for not picking up my charger, only to find it near the fridge. Why was it there? Your guess is as good as mine.

I had my share of pregnancy-induced meltdowns, one of which involved a full-blown fight over whether we should eat at home or go out. Spoiler: I didn't want either option.

My days were filled with anxiety—was I doing enough? Was I doing too much? Could I protect this baby from everything, including my own doubts and fears? Would we be good at it? Would our relationship change after the baby? We didn't have all the answers, but we had faith that we'd get through it together. And that was enough. But amidst it all, one thing was clear: this little peanut had already stolen our hearts.

A New Rhythm: Ryan's Patience and My Calmer Second Trimester

As my pregnancy journey continued, something unexpected happened: by the time I entered my second trimester, Ryan and I began to find a rhythm that worked for both of us. He had learned to understand me better—an achievement considering my emotional rollercoaster—and I found myself growing calmer as my body settled into its new state of being. Looking back, it was like the chaos of the first trimester was slowly melting away, replaced by a slightly more peaceful sense of reality. It wasn't all roses, but we were getting better at navigating the ups and downs together.

Ryan had been nothing but supportive from the moment we found out we were expecting, but during the first trimester, my mood swings often got the better of me. One minute I wanted him by my side constantly, and the next, I wanted to be left completely alone. I would snap at him over the smallest things—like putting the wrong kind of peanut butter on my sandwich or breathing too loudly (yes, *breathing*). To his credit, Ryan never lost his cool. Instead, he patiently tried to figure out what I needed, even when I didn't know it myself.

By the second trimester, though, a switch flipped. I started to gain a little more control over my emotions and began to focus on preparing for what was coming next. I realised that this wasn't just about getting through the day-to-day discomfort or the hormonal surges—it was about mentally and emotionally preparing to become a mother. That realisation brought a kind of calm I hadn't expected. Instead of fighting my body or my emotions, I leaned into the experience, accepting that it was okay to feel vulnerable and anxious. This helped me ease into the changes with a little more grace.

The Power of Affirmations

One thing that helped me tremendously during this time was discovering pregnancy affirmations. I had always been a bit sceptical of these kinds of things—you know, the "look in the mirror and tell yourself you're a goddess" kind of stuff—but as I struggled with the anxieties and fears of pregnancy, I was willing to try anything to keep my mind in a positive place. And to my surprise, it actually worked.

I began listening to pregnancy affirmations every morning, especially those that focused on strength, calmness, and confidence. There's something incredibly powerful about starting your day by affirming that your body is strong, capable, and designed to carry life. Hearing those words over and over again helped me reframe my thinking. Instead of focusing on the things I *couldn't* do, like certain exercises or eating my favourite sushi, I started focusing on what I *was* doing: nurturing and growing a little human inside me.

The affirmations became a form of mental training. I would sit quietly and repeat them to myself: "My body is strong, my baby is safe, and I am prepared for this journey." Slowly but surely, these mantras helped calm my anxieties. They gave me a sense of control when everything felt so uncertain. I found myself relaxing more, and Ryan noticed too. I wasn't snapping at him as often, and when I did, I was quicker to apologise. We were getting better at communicating, understanding each other, and being a team.

The Joy of Moving Again

Around the middle of my second trimester, I was finally cleared to start exercising again. To say I was overjoyed would be an understatement. After months of worrying about my physical strength and not being able to move the way I used to, I was itching to get back into some sort of routine. The thought of getting stronger, not just for myself but for my baby, filled me with a sense of purpose.

I started slowly, with light stretching and walking. I was determined to build my strength gradually, and every small step felt like a victory. Soon, I added squats to my routine, focusing on my lower body to prepare for the physical demands of labour. Upper body strength became a priority too—after all, I'd need strong arms to carry my little one once they arrived.

As I exercised, I felt a new kind of connection with my body. It wasn't just about getting fit; it was about preparing for the monumental task of giving birth. Each squat, each lift, each stretch reminded me that my body was capable of incredible things. And with every passing day, I felt more confident in my ability to handle what was coming.

Of course, there were moments of self-doubt. Was I doing enough? Was it safe to exercise? What if I pushed too hard? But each time those doubts crept in, I returned to my affirmations. "My body is strong. My baby is safe." And just like that, the fear would subside, replaced by a sense of peace and determination.

The 20-Week Anomaly Scan: A Rollercoaster of Nerves and Cheesecake

Just as I was beginning to settle into the rhythm of pregnancy, the 20-week anomaly scan loomed on the horizon like a dark cloud. This was the big one—the scan that would check for any abnormalities and ensure that our baby was developing as expected. Needless to say, the nerves were off the charts.

Ryan and I went to the ultrasound appointment feeling equally excited and terrified. I lay on the examination table, staring at the ceiling, trying to calm my racing heart. The technician applied the cold gel to my belly, and we waited for the first glimpse of our baby.

There it was—our little one on the screen, looking as perfect as ever. But, as it turned out, our baby was a bit camera-shy. Throughout the entire scan, it kept covering its face with its tiny hands, as if to say, "No paparazzi, please!" What should have been a quick 30-minute scan turned into a three-hour ordeal. The technician had to get clear images of the baby's face and certain organs, but our little one was stubbornly refusing to cooperate.

We tried everything. I walked around the clinic, did a few light stretches, and even ate a whole slice of cheesecake to get the baby to move. Nothing. Our sweet little one was perfectly content hiding from the world. Eventually, after what felt like an eternity, the technician was able to get the images she needed.

The results were mostly clear, but one level came back borderline high. Naturally, I freaked out. Even though the doctor assured us that it wasn't anything too concerning and gave me medication to manage it, I couldn't help but worry. Pregnancy had turned me into a professional overthinker. Every little thing felt like the end of the world. But I reminded myself that I was doing everything I could to keep my baby healthy and safe.

Dreams, Decisions and Future Plans

Around this time, Ryan and I began discussing our future. He had always wanted to pursue his master's degree abroad, and now that we were expecting a child, the conversation took on a new sense of urgency. We knew that raising a baby would come with financial challenges, and Ryan's advanced education would be key to providing the kind of life we wanted for our little one.

We decided to have an honest conversation with our families about Ryan's plans. To our relief, they were incredibly supportive. Both of our parents understood the importance of Ryan's goals and were ready to stand by us through whatever challenges lay ahead. It was a huge weight off.

Our shoulders to know that we had their blessing and support as we moved forward with our plans. While there was a lot of uncertainty about how everything would pan out—balancing a newborn with Ryan's studies, potentially moving abroad, and the countless other unknowns—we felt confident that we were on the right path.

We knew the road ahead wouldn't be easy, but the clarity we gained during those conversations gave us the reassurance we needed. We could pursue our dreams while also preparing for parenthood. With a solid support system behind us, we began to focus on the more immediate future: getting ready for the arrival of our little one.

Breaking News at Our Usual Spot: A Bittersweet Shift Abroad

It's funny how some places become the backdrop for life's biggest moments, and for us, our usual hangout spot had become exactly that—a place where news was broken, and life-changing conversations unfolded. This time, it wasn't any different, though the news we had to share brought with it a bittersweet mix of emotions.

As we sat in the car, our routine chit-chat unfolded—talking about office plans, job changes, and the usual day-to-day updates. But this time, there was something bigger hovering in the background, something we knew would shift everything. I turned to Meher, feeling a knot in my stomach, and said, "We have something important to share."

With anticipation and a slight nervousness in her eyes, she waited as Ryan and I exchanged a glance. And then, we said, "In the next few months, we'll be shifting abroad for Ryan's education."

For a split second, her face lit up with excitement—she was genuinely thrilled for us, knowing how big this opportunity was. But as the words sank in, reality hit. We weren't just moving to a different city; we were heading to a completely different country, with a time zone separating us and all the usual comforts of being just a call or drive away. The sparkle of excitement in her eyes softened as the sadness set in.

It wasn't just the physical distance that struck us all, but the emotional reality too. We had been through everything together for so many years—celebrations, heartbreaks, triumphs, and failures—and now, this chapter of our lives would be written from opposite sides of the world. The laughter we shared took on a more nostalgic tone, as we all knew this wasn't just a change in geography, but a shift in the dynamics of our friendship too.

Meher, being the strong, bubbly person she is, held it together. She was genuinely happy for us, but beneath that, the sadness was evident. None of us said it outright, but we knew this would mark the beginning of a new phase—one where our worlds would be connected more by memories and messages than spontaneous lunch dates and car talks.

As we drove away from our spot that day, it wasn't just the road that stretched ahead of us, but the realisation that life was changing, and though we would be apart, our friendship, built on decades of love and laughter, would always find its way to endure.

The Insta-Mom Life

Somewhere between the cravings and the chaos, I found solace in sharing my journey with the world. I started an Instagram page called *momandbabyorder*, documenting my pregnancy and connecting with other moms. I created content that was funny and relatable. In a few months, I grew to 3,000 followers.

Today? Over 38,000. I collaborated with well-known brands and built a community where moms could laugh, cry, and vent about the absurdity of pregnancy and motherhood. Who knew pregnancy would turn me into a social media mogul?

Preparing for Baby's Arrival: The Fun and the Frenzy

By the end of the second trimester, the reality of impending parenthood started to hit us hard. It was no longer some distant, abstract idea – it was happening, and it was happening soon. Suddenly, there was so much to do, and time seemed to be slipping through our fingers.

First up was creating a baby registry. I had no idea how many things a tiny human needed until I started putting the list together. Between cribs, strollers, diapers, clothes, bottles, and countless other baby essentials, I felt like I was drowning in options. Should we go for the minimalist crib or the one that came with all the bells and whistles? Did we need a diaper bag that looked fashionable, or was functionality more important? Every decision felt monumental.

Ryan, on the other hand, was much more laid-back about the whole thing. He trusted my judgement when it came to choosing what we needed, but that didn't stop him from chiming in with the occasional opinion. "Do we really need a baby monitor that connects to our phones?" he asked one day. "Can't we just check on the baby the old-fashioned way?" I rolled my eyes, knowing full well that once the baby arrived, he'd be the one glued to that app, watching every little movement.

After finalising the registry, we moved on to the more serious task of booking the hospital room. We toured several options, weighing the pros and cons of each facility. Ryan was meticulous, asking about everything from the safety protocols to the availability of lactation consultants. I was more focused on the comfort factor—did the rooms feel welcoming? Would I feel at ease here during labour? In the end, we found a hospital that ticked all the boxes, and we both felt a sense of relief knowing that at least one big decision was out of the way.

Next on the list was planning my maternity photoshoot. This was something I had been looking forward to from the moment I found out I was pregnant. I wanted to capture this beautiful, transformative time in my life—the glow, the growing bump, the anticipation of meeting our baby. We spent hours scrolling through Pinterest, looking for inspiration. Should we go for a nature-themed shoot or something more urban and chic?

The Countdown Begins

As the months went on, I continued to bond with my little one. I talked to my belly, played music for the baby, and did everything I could to prepare for this new chapter in our lives. Before I knew it, we were in the home stretch. The third trimester was winding down, and I was both terrified and excited for what was to come. Ryan and I spent our evenings snuggled up, dreaming about our future as parents, wondering what our little one would be like, and laughing at how clueless we still felt.

The Baby Shower Extravaganza

Then began the preparations for the **grand baby shower ceremony**. Oh, what a production it was! The venue suggestions flew faster than we could write them down. Should it be at a fancy hall, the backyard, or my parents' place? Every detail needed attention—from the guest list to the saree I would wear, to the decor that had to match said saree. And of course, the pièce de resistance – **the lad was**. For the uninitiated, these are Parsi sweets made from boondi and shaped into little cones of sugary goodness. Fifty boxes were to be painstakingly identical, each adorned with a "Thank You" sticker from Ryan and me. By the day before the event, we were buried in boxes, frantically ironing clothes, and sending polite-yet-anxious reminders to the makeup artist and photographer. The countdown was real.

On the day of the shower, I was dressed to the nines, makeup on point, and ready to conquer the world—or at least the ceremony. We reached the venue, where my mother and mother-in-law, along with a squad of married women, performed the traditional ceremony. Ryan and I then had our mini photoshoot (obviously!), complete with a special video where all the guests gave their best wishes for our little one. We ended the day by cutting cake, laughing with friends, and collapsing into bed with sore feet.

The Quest for The Perfect Maternity Photoshoot

The next few weeks were dedicated to searching for the *perfect* maternity photographer because, of course, if you're growing a human, you might as well make it look artsy. Ryan and I headed to the studio for our indoor shoot—Ryan in an olive green shirt and khaki pants, and me in a deep rust-coloured voluminous gown that screamed goddess energy. The shoot was spectacular! I was basically living my modelling dream, with the photographer telling me how to pose, which angle to look at, and how to work my pregnancy glow. After that, we quickly changed outfits and headed to a peaceful garden for our outdoor shoot. Ryan sported a denim shirt and tan pants, while I twirled around in a pink voluminous dress, pretending to be a Disney princess. After an hour of posing and taking mushy, Pinterest-worthy pictures, I was DONE. My legs were aching, and all I needed was a hot bath and a foot massage.

Third Trimester Drama: Enter The Foot Swelling!

One of the **many joys** of the third trimester? Swollen feet. After we got home from the photoshoot, I dipped my aching feet in warm salt water, feeling like I had aged a hundred years overnight. And yet, despite the discomfort, everything was still going *too* perfectly. Cue the universe throwing in a plot twist at 34 weeks.

The 34-Week Scare: Drama Unfolds!

I had just finished my daily exercise (yes, I was still trying to be Superwoman), and suddenly, after lunch, I felt cramps. "No big deal, probably Braxton Hicks," I thought. But by 6 PM, these cramps had evolved into something **very** uncomfortable and happening at regular intervals. I called my gynaecologist, who calmly informed me, "Head to the hospital *now*, this could be labour."

Labour?! At 34 weeks?! Ryan and I freaked out, sprinting around the house like headless chickens. Was this really happening? Were we about to meet our baby *tonight?* Ryan grabbed me, rushed us to the hospital, and once there, I was unceremoniously whisked into the labour room—without Ryan, because of *course* hospital rules forbade him from being by my side. With only 10% battery left on my phone, I was barely able to communicate with him. I was in **full panic mode**.

The nurse did her best to keep Ryan updated, but it wasn't the same. The doctor performed a non-stress test on the baby, then an internal examination, and finally told me I had a **short cervix**, a condition that can cause premature labour. She prescribed steroid injections to help the baby's lungs develop and medications to slow down the labour. Suddenly, I was told our baby might end up in the NICU for 15 days if born now.

NICU?! 15 days?! I was officially in meltdown mode. I desperately wanted Ryan with me, but he wasn't allowed inside. I clung to my faith, praying for the baby's safety while Ryan paced outside, blaming himself for being so strict with my exercise routine, thinking that maybe it was his fault. Spoiler alert: it wasn't. My condition was genetic, but try telling that to a dad-to-be in full freak-out mode.

I stayed overnight for observation, with only my mom and Mommy B allowed to visit me intermittently. Poor Ryan had to go home. For the next 12 hours, I was alone, praying for our baby's safety and wishing Ryan could be with me. When he was finally allowed in at 6 AM the next day, we both broke down into tears, hugging and kissing, apologising to each other and our baby for all the stress. Thankfully, we were sent home that afternoon, but I was now on **strict bed rest** for three weeks. No exercise, no socialising – just me, confined to my room, binge-watching TV and praying.

The Waiting Game: Deals With the Baby!

Those three weeks felt like an eternity. Ryan worked from home and prepared for his IELTS exam while I lay there, making daily deals with our baby. "Just stay in there until Daddy finishes his exam, okay?" Behzad had to travel for work, and we were all on edge, worried she might miss the birth. I was convinced our baby was going to make its grand entrance on Ryan and my anniversary, especially when I started feeling contractions the night before. **Anniversary baby?** Turns out, it was another case of Braxton Hicks.

On our actual anniversary, we had a cosy dinner at home with our parents, watching an India-Pakistan cricket match and taking *way* too many photos. It was a perfect night, albeit filled with a little bit of fear—because our baby was running the show, and we had no idea what would happen next.

The Big Finale

As the due date approached, so did Ryan's IELTS exam, and with it came **peak anxiety levels**. Between the impending labour, the thought of moving abroad, and his exam, Ryan's paranoia hit new heights. He began doubting whether he'd be a good father—whether he could bond with the baby, love it enough, and handle the responsibilities. We had one blowout argument that escalated into a full-blown drama, though I can't for the life of me remember what started it.

Then came the day of Ryan's exam, and we made one last deal with our baby— "Just stay inside until Daddy finishes his test, and then you can come out whenever you like." Miraculously, it worked! Ryan completed his exam, and we were back to eagerly waiting for our baby's arrival.

Now that I was full-term, I resumed my walks, squats, and exercises, determined to "squat this baby out" of me. I even got back to work, helping with Behzad's brand by creating content around pregnancy. We filmed podcasts and videos, wrapping things up before my official maternity leave. All that was left to do was wait.

The Final Countdown: A Prayer for Our Baby

Every night, we prayed for a healthy baby, thanking God for guiding us through the scare. We knew that whenever our little one decided to arrive, we'd be ready, armed with love, prayers, and a whole lot of humour to get us through.

Valuable Lessons Learned

One of the most profound lessons I learned during this phase of pregnancy is the importance of surrendering control and embracing the unpredictability of life. As someone who thrives on planning and having things go a certain way, pregnancy was a humbling experience that reminded me how little control I truly have over certain aspects of my life. No matter how much I prepared or anticipated, there were moments—like the exhausting five-hour ultrasound ordeal—where things didn't go according to plan. And that's okay.

Through this journey, I discovered the value of flexibility and trust. I had to learn to trust my body, trust the process, and most importantly, trust that things would work out as they were meant to. This lesson in surrender helped me become more patient, more present, and ultimately more accepting of the unknown.

Additionally, this chapter of my life taught me the significance of partnership. Ryan and I became stronger as a couple, learning to support and lean on each other through every challenge and triumph. It showed me that sometimes, strength lies not in being able to do everything perfectly but in being able to ask for help, share the load, and find joy in the journey together.

In the end, pregnancy wasn't just about bringing new life into the world – it was also about growing as a person, letting go of old expectations, and embracing the unexpected with grace.

A Note from Present Me to 20-Year-Old Me

Dear 20-Something-Year-Old Me,

Hey, there! It's me, a bit older and hopefully a little wiser. I wanted to take a moment to write you a note as you're navigating the wild, exhilarating, and sometimes chaotic journey of pregnancy. I know things feel a bit overwhelming right now, and you might be wondering how you're going to handle all the changes coming your way. So, here's a bit of advice from someone who's been there:

First off, breathe. I know it's easier said than done, but take a deep breath and remind yourself that it's okay to not have everything perfectly planned out. Life, especially when it comes to something as monumental as bringing a new life into the world, is full of surprises. Embrace the unexpected, and don't stress over things you can't control. It's in these moments of uncertainty that you'll find your true strength and resilience.

Remember, it's okay to feel anxious and overwhelmed. You're doing something incredible, and it's natural to have doubts and fears. It's all part of the journey. But also, don't forget to find joy in the small moments—like those tender kicks, the excited anticipation of each ultrasound, and the love that surrounds you. These moments are precious and will become some of your most cherished memories.

I want you to know that it's perfectly fine to lean on others. Ryan is there for you, and together, you'll figure out how to navigate this new chapter. Trust in each other and communicate openly. You'll find that your relationship will grow stronger through this shared experience.

Also, don't be too hard on yourself. You're doing your best, and that's more than enough. There will be days when you feel exhausted, and that's okay. Allow yourself to rest and recharge. Remember that self-care isn't a luxury; it's a necessity.

Lastly, embrace the journey with all its highs and lows. There will be challenging moments, but there will also be extraordinary joys. Your life is about to change in ways you can't even imagine, and while it may seem daunting, it's also going to be incredibly rewarding.

So, hang in there. You've got this. And when things get tough, just remember you're stronger than you think, and you're not alone.

With love and encouragement,

Present Me

Chapter 9
Meeting Our Blessing

From youthful doubts to a confident stance,
She embraced her past with a grateful glance,
From sleepless nights to lessons learned,
Her path was shaped by each twist and turn.
With baby steps and moments grand,
She found her strength, took a stand.
The decade's end, a bittersweet cheer,
Marked her growth and conquered fear.

The First Signs of Labour

On the morning of May 5th, 2024, I woke up at around 7 a.m., as usual, to rush to the bathroom. But something was different this time. As I peered down, I noticed a brownish discharge. I froze. My mind raced. Was this it? The moment I had been anticipating for nine long months? But wait! I wasn't due for another 2 weeks!

I rushed out of the bathroom and immediately informed Ryan, my heart pounding as I realised that this could be the day. We ran to tell my in-laws, excitement and nervousness flooding the room. There was no time to waste. I spoke to my doctor, who confirmed that I should head to the hospital immediately.

As we prepared to leave, Ryan and I shared a special moment. We made a sweet video, welcoming our baby into the world, expressing how much we already loved them. Before walking out the door, we snapped one last photograph of just the two of us—our final moments as a couple before we would become parents.

The Drive to The Hospital

The drive to the hospital felt surreal. My mind was swirling with so many emotions—fear, happiness, anxiety, and anticipation. Every minute felt like it carried a mix of excitement and uncertainty. What was labour going to feel like? How was everything going to unfold?

As we arrived at the hospital, the staff quickly whisked me into a room for a non-stress test. The machine confirmed I was indeed in labour, but to my surprise, I felt no real pain. No strong contractions, no intense cramping. My body was gearing up, but it seemed to be taking its time. After consulting with the doctor, I was advised to go home and return once the contractions started feeling like period cramps and were two hours apart.

Back Home, Bouncing Through Labour

Going home felt strange. We had thought we'd be holding our baby by the end of the day, but it seemed we had more waiting to do. Instead of panicking, we embraced the time we had left. Ryan and I had a good lunch together, laughed, and even joked about the situation. We spent the afternoon watching YouTube videos on ways to accelerate labour, hoping to give things a little nudge.

I spent over an hour bouncing on the birthing ball, determined to get things moving. A warm shower followed, which helped me relax and soothe my body, knowing that soon, things would get much more intense. Sure enough, by 7:30 p.m., the contractions started to become more regular, and I knew it was time to head back to the hospital.

The Long Night Begins

Once we arrived at the hospital, they performed another non-stress test, and it was clear that things were progressing slowly. I was only 2 cm dilated. I could feel the anxiety creeping in, knowing that labour could take many hours – or even days.

By 11 p.m., things started to intensify. The contractions hit hard, and I was exhausted, not from labour but from the anticipation of what was to come. My body was tired, my mind was on overdrive, but the pain was unrelenting. Despite the exhaustion, sleep was not an option, as each contraction took my breath away.

Ryan was by my side the whole time, holding my hand and offering endless support. I don't think I've ever squeezed his hand so tightly in my life. By 1:30 a.m. on 6th May 2024, my water broke. The pain was excruciating, each contraction more unbearable than the last. I kept praying, asking Jesus to stay by my side. I had no choice but to surrender to the process, letting go of control and trusting that my body and God would guide me through it.

Hunger Strikes At 3 AM

In the midst of all the pain, a wave of hunger hit me at 3 a.m. I hadn't eaten in hours, and my body was running on fumes. I sent Ryan on a mission to find food in the hospital, and after a 30-minute search, he returned triumphantly with a slab of chocolate. It wasn't much, but it was exactly what I needed to muster up the strength to keep going.

Despite the chocolate, I was utterly drained. I couldn't bear the pain any longer, so at 4 a.m., after much pleading, I was given an epidural. The relief was instant. For the first time in hours, I was able to relax, and for the next three hours, I actually slept.

The Final Stretch

At 7 a.m., the doctor returned with an update: I was 7 cm dilated, and the baby was ready to arrive in about an hour. A mixture of relief and anxiety washed over me. I had been in labour for over 24 hours, and though the epidural gave me some relief, the next part would be the hardest—delivery.

As the time approached, I could feel my body growing weaker from exhaustion, but the pain was still there, simmering beneath the surface. Suddenly, all the monitors around me began beeping. My heart dropped. The baby's heartbeat had decreased because, in my exhaustion, I had subconsciously stopped breathing. The staff immediately put me on oxygen, and slowly, everything returned to normal. It was a scare, but I was more determined than ever to bring our baby into the world safely.

Time To Push

Then came the moment I had been both dreading and preparing for—pushing. With each contraction, I had to muster all my strength and push with everything I had. Ryan was my rock through it all, encouraging me, holding my hand, and helping me breathe through the pain. His calm energy gave me the willpower to keep going.

After an hour of pushing, Ryan saw the baby's head and excitedly exclaimed, "It looks like a small hairy ball!" The entire room burst into laughter, a much-needed break in the tension.

But soon, things grew more intense. It was getting harder and harder to push, and my doctor informed me that she might need to use a suction cup to help pull the baby out. Ryan, ever the jokester, reminded me that he was born with the help of a suction cup, making me laugh even through the pain. But I wasn't having it. Determined, I yelled, "No! I don't want suction! I'll push this baby out!"

At that moment, a senior labour nurse climbed onto the bed, positioning herself behind me. She pushed down on my abdomen with such force that it felt like my ribs were going to break. It was the most intense moment of my life, but then, with one final push—**pop**—out slid our baby girl.

Our Blessing Arrives

She was a healthy 6-pound baby with the most peculiar cry I had ever heard—a sound I knew I would never forget. As they placed her on my chest, all the pain and exhaustion faded into the background. She was perfect. Her tiny body rested on mine as we shared that first precious moment together. Ryan kissed me, and both of us were overcome with tears of joy.

I couldn't believe it. After all the months of fear, anticipation, and countless worries, our baby girl was here, healthy and beautiful. Ryan cut the umbilical cord, and the nurses took her to clean her up and run their checks. Watching him hold her for the first time, I felt a deep sense of peace. If anything ever happened to me, I knew she would be safe in his arms. He had proven over the last 24 hours that I didn't need anyone else—Ryan was all I needed.

The First Look: A Mini Me

When they handed our baby back to me, I looked at her closely, taking in every tiny feature. She was a mini version of me—those beautiful wide eyes, courtesy of Ryan, a tiny button nose, and perfectly formed bow lips. A deep dimple graced her chin, and a small mop of curly, matted black hair covered her head.

I was in awe. She was everything I had dreamed of and more. It was surreal to think that this little being had been growing inside me all these months, and now she was finally in my arms.

The Emotional Reunion

Once we were settled into our room, my parents arrived. The moment they laid eyes on their granddaughter, I could see the emotion written all over their faces. They hugged me tightly, and I could feel their overwhelming pride and love. Holding their first granddaughter in their arms, their joy was palpable. I had never seen my parents look so happy.

Ryan, too, was glowing with pride. Over the last 24 hours, he had shown immense grace and strength. His love for me had only deepened through this experience. Watching him with our daughter, my heart swelled with gratitude for the man I had married. He had been my anchor through labour, and now, as a father, he was stepping into a new role with such natural ease.

A Moment of Perfection

As I lay in the hospital bed, holding my baby girl in my arms, I reflected on the last 24 hours. It had been one of the hardest days of my life, but it had also been the most rewarding. What

I had feared for nine long months was finally behind me, and I had triumphed. My reward was this beautiful, perfect little girl who looked so much like me.

In that moment, life felt perfect. I had my baby, I had Ryan, and I had the support of my family. I whispered a prayer of thanks to Jesus, who had been with me through every contraction, every fear, and every moment of joy. I thanked Him for blessing me with the best husband and child I could ever ask for.

Our journey as parents had just begun, but as I looked down at our mini me, I knew we were ready for whatever came next. She was our greatest adventure yet.

The Moment Meher Became Masi: A Bond Beyond Blood

The first time Meher came to visit after we brought our daughter home was one of those moments that will forever be etched in my heart. From the second she stepped into our home, her eyes were wide with excitement, eager to meet the little bundle of joy we had all been waiting for. She had anticipated our daughter's arrival just as much as we had, and the moment she finally held her "precious peanut" in her arms, the emotion overwhelmed her.

As she gazed down at our daughter's tiny, delicate face, her eyes welled up with tears. It was as if all the waiting, all the excitement, and all the love she had already felt for our little girl came rushing out at once. Meher, usually the loud, bubbly one, was now soft and tender, rocking our daughter gently and whispering sweet words to her. She kept calling her "my precious darling," speaking to her as if they shared a connection that had been there from the start.

And then it happened—our daughter, in all her innocence, gave Meher the cutest little smile. It was as if she knew, in that magical moment, that Meher wasn't just any visitor or friend, but someone incredibly special. The joy and pride I felt were indescribable. Watching them together, I realised that our daughter wasn't just my baby—she was Meher's baby too, in a way only the truest of friendships can create.

In that simple, yet profound exchange, I saw that our daughter had not only a best friend in Meher but a second mother, a confidant, and a protector for life. There was no doubt in my mind—this bond was something extraordinary, and it would grow just as strong as the one Meher and I shared.

The Aftermath: Total Chaos Ensues

The next month was, in one word, **chaos**. Forget the picture-perfect scenes of new parenthood you see on Instagram—the matching pyjamas, the serene baby sleeping in your arms. Nope, none of that. Instead, we were plunged headfirst into a never-ending loop of *what felt like madness*. We brought our baby girl home, and from the very first night, all hell broke loose.

Every two hours, like clockwork, we were up—feeding, burping, changing diapers, pumping, and trying to rock this tiny human back to sleep. By the time we managed to doze off ourselves, round two would start all over again. No breaks, no mercy. Honestly, I didn't know how people survived this without completely losing their minds. We were zombies, barely functioning.

Ryan and I had never looked more like a pair of exhausted, sleep-deprived raccoons in our entire lives. Our eyes were bloodshot, our hair unwashed, and showers became a luxury we could only dream of. Every time I laid down, I'd hear that tiny *cry*, signalling another feeding, another diaper change. I swear, at one point, I thought, *"This is it. This is how it ends. We'll never sleep again."*

The Struggle Is Real: Postpartum Hits Hard

On top of all the chaos, I was also hit with postpartum depression. It came out of nowhere, like a freight train. One minute I was just tired, and the next, I was second-guessing every single thing I did. I felt like the *worst mom on the planet.* My baby girl seemed calm and peaceful in everyone's arms but mine. Whenever she was with me, she'd fuss and cry, and I began to think, *what am I doing wrong?*

Physically, I was in agony. The stitches from the delivery were healing slowly, and every movement felt like I was being stabbed. I couldn't sit comfortably, let alone hold my baby without feeling some sort of pain. All I wanted was to be the best mom I could be, but my body felt like it was betraying me, and mentally, I was unravelling.

Super-Dad to The Rescue: Ryan's Night Shift

Ryan, bless his soul, was a rock. He took over the night shifts as much as he could, letting me rest, or at least attempt to. But even with his help, the exhaustion was getting to both of us. I was still trying to process the birth trauma I'd gone through—flashbacks of that night would hit me out of nowhere, and I couldn't shake the feeling that I'd been through some kind of battle.

There were times when I'd snap at Ryan, yelling at him that he wasn't doing things right. In my mind, *I* was the mom, *I* knew how to do everything perfectly (even though I had no idea what I was doing). Of course, Ryan would lose it sometimes too. We were both hanging on by a thread, trying to figure out this new life while sleep-deprived and overwhelmed.

At one point, I caught him crying in secret. He didn't want me to see, but I knew. He was struggling too, and neither of us knew how to talk about it. The trauma, the physical pain, the emotional whirlwind—it was all too much.

Panic Attack Central: My Breakdown

And then it happened—my complete and total breakdown. One day, after what felt like a never-ending cycle of sleepless nights and emotional roller coasters, I broke down in hysterics. Full-on ugly crying. I couldn't breathe, my chest felt like it was going to explode, and I spiralled into a full-blown panic attack.

Ryan rushed over, trying to calm me down, but I was beyond reach. I just kept crying, thinking *how could I love my daughter so much and still feel like this?* The guilt was crushing me. I adored our daughter with all my heart, but I was also trapped in this dark cloud of depression and anxiety. It was like living in two different worlds at once—one filled with love and joy, the other with fear and sadness.

Medication, Help and Healing

That was the moment I realised I needed help. This wasn't something I could fix on my own. I started taking anti-anxiety medication, and it made a world of difference. Slowly, I began to feel like myself again. I could breathe. I could *function*. I could be the mom I wanted to be without feeling like I was drowning in my own mind.

Ryan, bless him, was my anchor. He had been there through every contraction, every sleepless night, every single breakdown. He is the best father anyone could ask for, and as much as I doubted myself, he never doubted me. We were both doing our best, even when it felt like our best wasn't enough.

Our Daughter: Our Perfect Little Miracle

As for our baby daughter? She was (and is) our perfect little miracle. Happy, gracious, and ever-thriving. Even through all the madness, I'd look at her and feel my heart swell with love. I knew we were in this together, as a family.

But wow—those first few weeks were an absolute *wild ride*. Looking back now, it's hard not to laugh at the total insanity of it all. Ryan and I somehow survived, and despite all the chaos, we grew stronger as a couple. Sure, we had our moments of snapping at each other, but we learned to lean on one another more than ever before.

This chapter of meeting our mini me was the start of a new life, one that was messy, beautiful, chaotic, and full of love. And honestly, I wouldn't trade a single sleepless night for anything in the world.

The Beauty in Chaos

As we emerged from the whirlwind of sleepless nights, endless nappy changes, and the emotional rollercoaster that came with welcoming our mini me, I realised that the chaos itself was a lesson. Becoming parents wasn't just about learning how to care for a newborn—it was about learning *about ourselves* in ways we never expected.

First, I learned to accept that perfection is an illusion. As much as I wanted to be the perfect mom, I had to let go of the idea that I needed to have all the answers. Parenthood is messy, unpredictable, and no one does it flawlessly. There's beauty in embracing the imperfections, knowing that every mistake is just another step in the learning process.

Ryan and I also learned the true meaning of partnership. There were moments of frustration, exhaustion, and even anger, but in the end, we became stronger together. We figured out how to support each other, not just as husband and wife, but as parents. Ryan showed me what true strength and love look like, and it deepened my respect and admiration for him in ways I can't put into words.

Most importantly, I learned that it's okay to ask for help. Whether it was leaning on Ryan during those tough nights, accepting my need for anti-anxiety medication, or allowing myself to cry when things became too much, asking for help doesn't make you weak. It makes you human.

Through the chaos, the tears, the laughter, and the sleepless nights, the biggest lesson I learned is that love—raw, imperfect, and unconditional—is what makes it all worth it. We are far from having everything figured out, but we have each other, and we have our beautiful little daughter. And that is more than enough.

A Note from Present Me to 20-Year-Old Me

Dear 20-Year-Old Me,

Buckle up, sweetheart, because the ride ahead is going to be wild. I know you think you've been through a lot already, but let me tell you—nothing prepares you for the beautiful chaos that is motherhood. I see you now, brimming with dreams, anxiety, and that relentless desire to control everything around you. Spoiler alert: You won't be able to control a damn thing—and that's okay.

You'll face moments that will test your patience, your strength, and your very idea of who you are. The perfect, put-together version of yourself that you're striving so hard to become? Let her go. There will be days when you'll be crying at 3 a.m., covered in spit-up, wondering if you'll ever get this parenting thing right. And guess what? You will. Not because you followed every rule in the book or because you magically became "the perfect mom," but because you loved with every ounce of your being. That love? It's what will get you through.

Ryan will be your rock. You'll see a side of him that will blow your mind – he'll show up in ways you didn't even know were possible. You'll both struggle, stumble, and snap at each other in the sleep-deprived haze, but together, you'll come out stronger. Trust him. Trust yourself.

Postpartum? Yeah, that's going to be rough. You're going to feel things you can't even explain right now—like loving someone so deeply it hurts, but also feeling lost in the whirlwind of it all. When you find yourself in those dark moments, remember you're not alone. Reach out, lean on those around you, and don't be afraid to ask for help.

Lastly, give yourself grace. You'll make mistakes. Lots of them. But every mistake is a lesson. Every meltdown is a reminder that you're human. And every single moment of pain, doubt, and joy will be worth it when you hold that little girl in your arms and realise that she's the best part of you.

You're going to be an amazing mom. And when the time comes, you'll see what I mean.

Love,

Future You (with more love, more mess, and way less sleep)

Chapter 10

From Clueless to Confident: Goodbye 20's

In the final chapter, she looks back with grace,
A decade's journey etched on her face,
Through laughter, tears and deep lessons,
Her journey shaped the soul she keeps.
From clueless days to confident nights,
She's found her path, her inner light.
With the past behind and a bright future,
She steps ahead, ready for new heights.

The time has come. The end of an era. My 20s are officially behind me, and I have to admit, I'm feeling a lot of things. Nostalgia? Check. Relief? Absolutely. And just a tiny bit of, "Shucks, what just happened?" Because let's be real, my 20s were nothing short of a dramatic rollercoaster that I barely survived—and yet, somehow, I wouldn't change a thing.

This decade was supposed to be where I "figured it all out," right? You know that cliché journey of self-discovery, finding love, achieving your career goals, and living out your wildest dreams. But if you were to rewind to my early 20s and ask that wide-eyed, hopelessly naive version of myself where she saw life going, her response would be... laughable.

Entering Adulthood: Fake It till You Make It

At the start of my 20s, I was practically a professional "fake adult." Sure, I thought I was grown. I moved out, had a bank account that barely held more than a few hundred bucks at any given moment, and acted like I knew what I was doing. Spoiler alert: I didn't. And it was painfully obvious to everyone except me. Whether it was juggling relationships, friends, and career decisions, I learned pretty quickly that adulthood isn't about having all the answers — it's about making peace with the fact that you never will.

I made terrible decisions – some hilariously bad, some cringe-worthy, and some that led to me dating two people at once (still can't believe I thought that was a good idea). But from each face-palm-worthy experience came lessons that began to shape me. It turns out, being an adult isn't about having it all together. It's about navigating the chaos and still showing up for yourself every day.

Self-Discovery And Identity: Embracing the Mess

Oh, the mess. The glorious mess of self-discovery. My early 20s were riddled with questions of identity. Who am I? What do I value? Why is everyone else seemingly thriving while I'm drowning in uncertainty? I stumbled through friendships that didn't serve me, clung to toxic relationships longer than I should have, and questioned my purpose more times than I can count.

But here's the thing: I found myself through the mess. Every mistake, every heartbreak, and every tear-soaked pillow pushed me closer to understanding who I truly was. I found God during this period, and it changed everything. Slowly, I began to let go of what was holding me back: friendships, habits, self-doubt. As I embraced the uncomfortable parts of my journey, I started to realise something: I was becoming the person I was always meant to be. Not perfect, not flawless, but real and unapologetically me.

Love, Loss and the Quest for Balance

As I moved through my 20s, I experienced love in all its confusing, complicated, beautiful forms. I met Ryan, my husband, and in him, I found a partner who saw the best in me even when I couldn't. But it wasn't always smooth sailing. We had our ups and downs, and let's not forget the chaotic transition into parenthood – where sleep became a distant memory, and we found ourselves juggling diapers, late-night feeds, and our sanity.

But through it all, we grew stronger together. Ryan was my anchor, my biggest cheerleader, and sometimes, the unfortunate target of my postpartum rage when I was sleep-deprived and barely functioning. We learned the hard way that relationships aren't about romance and butterflies – they're about showing up for each other, even when you're both falling apart.

The Lessons That Changed Me

As I bid farewell to my 20s, I can't help but reflect on the biggest lessons that shaped me.

- **Perfection is overrated.** Seriously, who was I kidding trying to be perfect? Life is messy, and that's where the magic happens.

- **You will survive your worst days.** There were times when I thought I wouldn't make it — times when the anxiety, depression, and heartache were too much to bear. But I did make it, and I came out stronger on the other side.

- **Ask for help.** Whether it was therapy, leaning on friends, or relying on Ryan, I learned that I don't have to do it all alone.

- **Surrender control.** If my 20s taught me anything, it's that life rarely goes according to plan. And that's okay. Learning to let go and trust the process was one of the hardest and most liberating things I ever did.

- **Celebrate the little victories.** Whether it was finally mastering the art of parallel parking or surviving my first day of labour, the small wins matter. They add up to something big.

- **Faith is everything.** Turning to God during my toughest moments gave me strength I didn't know I had. My faith carried me through when nothing else could.

A Note from Present Me to 20-Year-Old Me

Hey you,

I know you're a bit of a mess right now — and I mean that in the most loving way possible. You're confused, scared, and probably second-guessing every decision you make. You're trying so hard to figure out who you are, where you're going, and what you're supposed to be doing with your life. It feels like everyone else has it all together, and you're the only one stumbling in the dark.

But guess what? It's all going to be okay. Better than okay, actually. Trust me, I know, because I'm living the future you're so worried about right now.

There's something else I need to tell you—something I wish you could understand now, but you'll learn soon enough. You don't have to carry the weight of the world on your shoulders. You've been trying to do everything on your own, to fix yourself, to make sense of the chaos, but you're not alone in this. God is with you, even in the moments when you feel most lost. And it's in the quiet, desperate prayers, when you surrender your fear and pain to Him, that you'll find the peace you've been searching for.

You'll come to realise that your strength doesn't come from your own efforts – it comes from leaning on God. He will be your rock when everything else feels uncertain. There will be times when you'll question everything, but He'll guide you through the storm. You'll find a deeper faith, one that will carry you through every trial, and that faith will transform you in ways you can't even imagine.

I wish I could sit with you and tell you that all the self-doubt, anxiety, and heartbreak will lead you to the woman you're meant to be. I know you're struggling, trying to please everyone, trying to fit into roles that don't feel quite right. You're making mistakes (some pretty hilarious ones), and you're probably feeling like you'll never get it together. But here's the truth: you're already on the right path, even if it doesn't feel like it.

You will stumble, you will fall, but you'll get back up every single time. You'll figure out who you are, and when you do, you'll be amazed by how strong, resilient, and beautiful you've become — not because of anything you did, but because God has been holding you through it all. You'll learn to love yourself in ways you never thought possible. And most importantly, you'll learn that you don't have to have it all figured out — life is an ever-evolving journey, and God's plan is bigger and better than anything you could ever dream.

There will come a time when you stop being that clueless girl searching for her place in the world. You'll become a woman who knows her worth, who stands tall in her own identity, and who has faith that guides her through every storm. You'll find a love that is real, deep, and unwavering – a love with a man who will be your partner through it all. You'll marry Ryan, and trust me, he will turn out to be everything you prayed for and more. He'll be your rock, your greatest support, and the love of your life.

And then, one day, you'll hold your beautiful baby girl in your arms. She will have your eyes, your smile, and yes, your fiery spirit. You'll look at her and realise that all the fear and doubt you had about motherhood were for nothing. You will be the best mom you can be, even on the days when you feel like you're failing. Because here's the secret: you won't fail. You'll learn, you'll grow, and you'll love her with a depth you didn't know existed — and with God's grace, you'll find the strength to be exactly what she needs.

I won't lie to you – it won't be easy. There will be sleepless nights, postpartum struggles, and moments when you think you're not enough. But you are enough. You always have been. And you'll come to understand that everything you've been through, all the highs and lows, have prepared you for this life that's more beautiful than you could have ever imagined.

So, stop worrying so much. Stop being so hard on yourself. Life is going to surprise you in the best ways possible. You're going to make it, and you're going to thrive. By the time you say goodbye to your 20s, you'll be saying hello to a woman who is confident, strong, and ready for whatever comes next. You'll be proud of who you've become, and you'll be grateful for every lesson learned along the way.

Through it all, remember this: you are never alone. God is always by your side, guiding you, shaping you, and holding you. He's brought you through every storm, and He'll keep doing it every single time.

I love you, and I'm so proud of the woman you've grown into. Keep going – the best is yet to come.

With love, faith and wisdom,

Your 30-Something Self

Conclusion: Goodbye, 20's. You Were Wild

As I sit here at the end of this chapter, it's bittersweet. Saying goodbye to my 20s feels like closing a book that had it all – drama, comedy, romance, and even a bit of tragedy. I laughed, I cried (a lot), and I grew in ways I never thought possible. This decade shaped me, stretched me, and sometimes nearly broke me. But most importantly, it transformed me.

If I could go back and do it all again—all the awkward moments, all the mistakes, all the sleepless nights—I would. Every experience, whether painful or joyous, brought me closer to the confident woman I am today. A woman who's still figuring it out but who knows she has the strength, the resilience, and the faith to take on whatever comes next.

What Comes Next?

As I step into the next decade of my life, I don't have all the answers. But I don't need to. My 20s taught me that it's okay to not have it all figured out, to embrace the chaos, and to trust that things will fall into place in their own time. I'm ready for whatever the 30s have in store – hopefully with a little more sleep and a lot more wisdom.

So, here's to the decade that gave me everything – heartbreaks, breakthroughs, friendships, faith, and the most life-changing experiences of all.

Goodbye, 20s. You were wild, chaotic, and wonderful. I'll never forget you.

Cue Drumroll — **And hello, 30s. Let's do this.**